CHILDREN'S INTERESTS IN READING

CHILDREN'S INTERESTS IN READING

ARTHUR MELVILLE JORDAN, Ph.D.
*Professor of Educational Psychology
in the University of North Carolina*

Revised and Brought Down to Date

CHAPEL HILL
THE UNIVERSITY OF NORTH CAROLINA PRESS
LONDON: HUMPHREY MILFORD
OXFORD UNIVERSITY PRESS
1926

First edition Copyright, 1921, By A. M. Jordan
Second edition Copyright, 1926, By A. M. Jordan

COMPOSED, PRINTED AND BOUND BY
The Collegiate Press
GEORGE BANTA PUBLISHING COMPANY
MENASHA, WISCONSIN

THIS BOOK WAS DIGITALLY PRINTED.

PREFACE

The present volume is an outgrowth of the author's previous work on "Children's Interests in Reading," now out of print. A new census of children's preferences has been taken in two high schools of North Carolina located in the cities of Greensboro and Charlotte. In all, 1559 additional boys and girls have been asked to write down five books and three magazines which they like very much. This material has been treated in precisely the same way as was that in the previous enquiry so that comparative data taken eight years apart are now available. Lists of most popular books and magazines were also constructed for each grade. All told then, nearly five thousand records, or forty thousand books and magazines, have been tabulated and classified.

It is a pleasure to acknowledge the assistance of others in this investigation. Carrie Nicholson Jordan classified the nearly twenty-five thousand books in the two investigations. This invaluable assistance has made it possible to include larger numbers of pupils in the censuses and to bring out this volume much earlier than otherwise would have been possible. Elmer H. Garinger, Principal of the Central High School of Charlotte and Fred Archer, Superintendent of City Schools at Greensboro were kind enough to have the questionnaire given to the high school pupils of their cities.

A. M. J.

TABLE OF CONTENTS

I. Introduction	1
a. Purpose	1
b. Methods	2
c. Review of former studies	4
d. Bibliography	12
II. Investigations in Libraries	14
a. Description of method	14
b. Tables of most popular books for boys and girls	20
c. Dicussion of interests of boys and girls by reviewing and analyzing the most used books	20
d. Summary	27
III. Results of Questionnaire 1917	29
a. Description of method	29
b. Tables of types of books	34
c. Lists of books arranged by age	35
d. Discussion of magazines	40
e. Lists of magazines arranged by age	44
f. Summary	48
IV. Results of Questionnaire 1925	52
a. Table of types of magazines. Boys. Girls	54
b. Percentage tables comparing choices of boys and girls in 1917 and in 1925	57
c. Lists of magazines found interesting	60
d. Lists of popular magazines comparing Greensboro and Charlotte	63
e. Percentage table of types of books with discussion	68
f. Lists of books from Greensboro and Charlotte arranged by age and by grade	74
g. Most popular books of both investigations	89
h. Summary and conclusion	90
V. Interpretation and attempted explanation of children's reading	93

CHILDREN'S INTERESTS IN READING

CHILDREN'S INTERESTS IN READING

CHAPTER I

INTRODUCTION

The abiding interest of school children in their subjects of study has for many years been one of the criteria of good instruction. In classes in literature this becomes a problem of peculiar interest. Unless the student turns to his literature with satisfaction there may be developed in him a distaste for that type of thing considered desirable; and if a distaste for, then a turning away from, and finally an almost complete forgetting of, all he has learned about the subject. If we could determine what the child's major interests are, be those interests good or bad, it would be possible to direct these forces along lines which are desirable. If not directly, at least indirectly, we could connect the school subject with his interests and show how it is related to them.

The importance of having boys and girls interested in books, stories, and poems cannot be overestimated; for their interest causes them to remember longer a story or poem studied and also creates a desire for more. Thus is there provided for the 'activity which leads to further activity,' the bone and marrow of the learning process.

For example, a boy twelve or thirteen years of age who is introduced to Stevenson's *Treasure Island* finds himself in a world to his own liking. He is surprised and pleased that a book of this type should be recommended by his teachers. Thus, the satisfaction which comes with reading such a book strengthens the connections between the situation, *reading*, and the response, *reading a book which is socially desirable.* In the second place, this satisfaction might lead him to search more closely other recommended books and possibly lead to a more extended interest in literature. Or, more specifically, the known interest in scouting and wars, as described by Altsheler, might be directed to an interest in the lives of our frontiersmen of national fame, and from these to a knowledge of history—"the lengthened shadows of the lives of great men!"[1]

Since books are constantly changing, it is as important to know the methods of discovering the interests of pupils as it is to know what those interests are. Sometimes when questioned directly, pupils will not put down the names of books actually liked, for there is always a deal of clandestine reading which no sort of questioning will discover; but since most of this type is of such a nature that it ought to be abandoned, its detection would be of little value.

There are two general ways of discovering these interests: the one, by questioning the pupil directly as to his likes and dislikes; the other, by watching carefully his withdrawal of books from libraries, the wearing out of copies in public libraries, and even the amount of wear of the library cards. Each is open to objection: The first, in that children frequently will not coöperate because they suspect you of some game or other, or else they like to joke and put down unheard of books; the second, because it is impossible to discover why the books were removed. None of these objections is completely valid. In a census of 3598 children, when their identity was veiled by requiring them to write their first names only, and when it was urged that we really did want to know what they liked, there were found only a few cases where the child failed to coöperate or where there was a discoverable conscious effort to deceive. In

[1] One of the most helpful books in this connection is S. A. Leonard's *Essential Principles of Teaching Reading and Literature* (Lippincott).

the case of withdrawals from libraries this one error did appear. In many libraries children are permitted to take out two books, but only one of these may be a story book. Children almost always want to withdraw the greatest possible number, so they take out a story book, then a second book, frequently for no other purpose than that they think they must get everything they can. This causes an enormous circulation of books which, I am convinced, from three months constant observation in children's rooms in public libraries, are not nearly so interesting as the circulation would indicate.

There are several methods of direct questioning of children. In one of these, types of reading such as "Stories of adventure, of travel, of great men, of great women, etc.,"[1] are submitted. This method fails somewhat because children do not always differentiate between the categories, and consequently each seems to have a larger percentage of interest than it actually contains. Again, such questions are used as: "What books have you read since school opened in September; which do you like best?"[2] "Do you take books from the library?" "What was the name of your last book?" "Why did you take it?"[3] "Who is your favorite author?"[4] etc. It is probably useless to ask a pupil in high school or in the grades why he likes a book. This is a difficult enough question for sophisticated grownups to answer. The answers to such questions certainly give no adequate notion of why children like certain books rather than others. Sometimes it is profitable to furnish a list of books and have the pupils check those they like and those they do not like. This

---

[1] Russell, J. E., and Bullock, R. W., "Some Observations of Children's Reading." *N.E.A. Proceedings*, 1897, 1015–21.
[2] Henderson, H. C., "Report on Child Reading." *Report of the Department of Public Instruction of New York.* II: 978–91 (1897).
[3] Vostrovsky, C., "Children's Taste in Reading." *Pedagogical Seminary*, VI: 523–38.
[4] Atkinson, F. W., "The Reading of Young People." *Library Journal*, XXXIII: 129–34 (1908).

method offers possibilities, particularly if there have been preliminary investigations.

Among the objective methods, records of withdrawals of books from libraries in which the children have complete freedom of choice furnish us with data which, if judiciously interpreted and followed up by actual observations of children in their selection of books and stories, may be of much value. In many ways this observation in children's libraries is the best method of all. It gives one an opportunity to see just how interested in books children may become. There are many of the beautifully illustrated books which children seek very eagerly. They sit and look at pictures sometimes for a half hour or an hour without being bored at all. In Chapter II a detailed account of the author's observations in libraries in and around New York City is given.

In concluding this chapter the findings of other studies on children's interests are summarized. There have been very few such studies in recent years. Indeed, most of the work was done several years ago, beginning about 1897 and continuing to 1909.[5]

The lists of books below, showing types of books liked by children, is taken from a report by H. C. Henderson. The study was made about 1896 to 1897. Many of these books are attractive to children even in the present day when there are so many books which appeal directly to children. These lists of books were compiled from answers which children gave to the question: "What books have you read since school opened in September (8 months)? Which did you like best?"

Books continuously popular between years 11–15 with boys and girls are:

---

[5] Recently there has been a renewal of attention to books found interesting to children. A notable illustration of this is "The Winetka Graded Book List" by Carleton Washburne and Mabel Vogel.

Boys	Girls
Black Beauty	Black Beauty
Uncle Tom's Cabin	Uncle Tom's Cabin
Life of Washington	Under the Lilacs
Little Men	Little Women
	Life of Washington
	Little Men

Books popular between years 11–12 and not later are:

Boys	Girls
Life of Washington	Life of Washington
Fairy Tales	Fairy Tales
Frank of the Gunboat	Sara Crewe
Juan and Juanita	Editha's Burglar
Five Little Peppers	Seven Little Sisters
Little Red Riding Hood	Little Red Riding Hood
Two Little Pilgrims' Progress	Gulliver's Travels
Hunters of the Ozarks	Two Little Pilgrims' Progress
The Lion of St. Marks	Life of Franklin
Frank of the Mountain	

Books popular between years 13–15 and not before are:

Boys	Girls
Building of a Nation	Lamplighter
Life of Lincoln	Life of Lincoln
History of the United States	Aunt Jo's Scrap Book
Swiss Family Robinson	Christmas Carol
Tom Sawyer	Wandering Jew
David Copperfield	Ben Hur
Count of Monte Christo	Elsie's Children
Last of the Mohicans	Scottish Chiefs
Castaway in the Cold	Ivanhoe
Poor Boys Who Became Famous	Nicholas Nickleby
Pilgrim's Progress	Beautiful Joe

The following table shows the choices of books of grammar grade pupils. The data are taken from three representative studies.

TABLE I

MOST POPULAR BOOKS AS SHOWN BY THREE STUDIES OF GRAMMAR GRADE PUPILS.

No. 1. Iowa City, Cedar Rapids, Council Bluffs, 1907. Frank O. Smith. *Ped. Sem.* 1907. Books selected voluntarily.
Pupils wrote as many as they pleased. First choices used.

6 CHILDREN'S INTERESTS IN READING

No. 2. West Boylston, Mass. Arthur P. Irving. *Ped. Sem.*, 1900.
"Name books that you have read and name those you liked best."
Seventh grade.

No. 3. Several Grammar Schools in Chicago. H. C. Henderson. N. Y.
State Report, 1897.
"What books have you read since school opened in September (8 mos.)? Which did you like the best?"
First choices used.

Author	Title	Study No.1 B	Study No.1 G	Study No.2 B	Study No.2 G	Study No.3 B	Study No.3 G
		385	573	61	60	1511	1475
Alger, H.	Works	25	14				
Alcott:	Series	20	80		22	27	139
Blackmore:	Lorna Doone	9	19				
Burnett:	Works	8	23	3	4	7	24
Carroll, L.:	Alice's Adventures in Wonderland	12	28				
Churchill:	The Crisis	11	48				
Clemens, S.L.	Works	35	19	6	1	7	5
Connor:	Works	166	27				
Defoe:	Robinson Crusoe	10	10	32	26	47	27
Dickens:	Works	15	35			1	11
Finley:	Elsie Dinsmore	8	53				
Fox:	Little Shepherd of Kingdom Come	10	39				
Heminway:	Bracebridge: Jack Harkaway Books	31	393				
Henty:	Works	56	11				
Hughes:	Tom Brown's School Days	16	7				
London:	Call of the Wild	40	10				
McCutcheon	Works	12	107				
Otis:	Toby Tyler	20	4				
Rice:	Works	40	29				
Saunders:	Beautiful Joe	31	64				
Scott:	Works	11	12				
Sewell:	Black Beauty	81	118	4	26	29	20
Sidney:	Margaret: Five Little Peppers	18	110	4	13	2	3
Stevenson:	Treasure Island	45	90				
Stowe:	Uncle Tom's Cabin	11	23	15	20	23	63
Wallace:	Ben Hur	6	15				5
Wister:	The Virginian	11	23				
Wyss:	Swiss Family Robinson	22	23	4	3	4	3
	Youth's Companion			30	38		

Longfellow:	Poems..................	5	9	12	17
Irving:	Rip Van Winkle...........	6	6		
Aldrich:	Peck's Bad Boy...........	7	0		
Lang:	Arabian Nights...........	1	6	2	5
Bunyan:	Pilgrim's Progress.........	1	6		
	Fairy Stories.............		7	17	25
Coffin:	Boys of '76...............			53	5
Brooks:	Life of Washington........			32	20
(Hill):	Little Red Riding Hood.....			2	19
Moore:	Life of Lincoln............			14	7
Burnett:	Little Pilgrims Progress.....			5	12
Aldrich:	American History..........			15	0
Andrews:	Seven Little Sisters.........			3	11
	Story of our Country.......			8	1
Coffin:	Building a Nation..........			7	2
	Sweet William............			2	7
D'Amicis:	Cuore...................			4	5
	Cinderella................			0	8
Cummins:	Lamplighter..............			1	6
Craik:	John Halifax..............			1	6
Baylor:	Juan and Juanita..........			7	0
Porter:	Scottish Chiefs............			13	3
Swift:	Gulliver's Travels..........			6	0
Dumas:	Count of Monte Christo.....			3	2
Bunyan:	Pilgrim's Progress.........			2	3
Franklin:	Life of Franklin...........			3	2
	Life of Daniel Boone.......			5	0
Scott:	Ivanhoe..................			3	2
Warner:	Wide, Wide World.........			0	5
Wiggin:	Birds' Christmas Carol.....			0	5

Table II gives the books most often chosen by high school pupils when an opportunity was given them to write down books which they liked.

Table II

Most Popular Books. High School Pupils.
As shown by three representative studies.

No. 1 Iowa City, Cedar Rapids, Council Bluffs, 1907, Frank O. Smith, *Ped. Sem., 1907.*
Books students selected.
Wrote as many as they pleased.
First choices used.

No.2 Iowa City and Fort Dodge, Ia., 1912. Roxanna E. Anderson. *Ped. Sem.*, 1912.
Number of books each month.
Books liked best. High School.
First choices used.

No.3 Various schools. Allan Abbott. *Sch. Rev.*, 1902.
List of 178 titles submitted to be evaluated.
Might add books they liked.
Returns not so good because students had the attitude of *required* reading. Books suggested by pupils.

		Study No.1		Study No.2		Study No.3	
Author	Title	B	G	B	G	B	G
		245	399	261	309	889	1589
Alcott:	Series....................		10		26		
Alger, H.:	Works....................	5	2	3			
Blackmore:	Lorna Doone..............	7	12	15	13		
Carroll:	Alice's Adventures in Wonderland................		5				
Churchill:	The Crisis.................	18	47	6	12		
Clemens:	Works....................	6	2	12			
Connor:	Works....................	9	14	17	12		
Defoe:	Robinson Crusoe...........	6	17				
Dickens:	Works....................	13	52	9	37	1	1
Finley:	Elsie Dinsmore Books.......		7				
Fox:	Little Shepherd of Kingdom Come...................	15	49	8	11		
Hemming:	Jack Harkaway Series.......	1	5				
Henty:	Works....................	17	1			1	
Hughes:	Tom Brown's School Days....	6	6				
London:	Call of the Wild............	28	8	34	6		
McCutcheon	Works....................		4				
Sidney:	Five Little Peppers..........	4	29				
Stevenson:	Treasure Island.............	6	7	81	28		
Stowe:	Uncle Tom's Cabin..........	20	32		5		
Wallace:	Ben Hur...................	10	12	5			1
Wister:	The Virginians.............	20	32	4			
	Nedra....................		8				
Jackson:	Ramona...................		4		20		
Cummins:	Lamplighter...............		3				
Roe:	Barriers Burned Away.......		3				
Dodge:	Hans Brinker..............			3	10		
Young:	Motor Boy Series...........			9			

INTRODUCTION

Rice:	Mrs. Wiggs of the Cabbage Patch..................	25		
Wiggin:	Rebecca of Sunnybrook Farm.	16		
Scott:	Ivanhoe...................	10	27	
Eliot:	Mill on the Floss............	5	30	
Eggleston:	Hoosier Schoolmaster.......	6	10	
Hale:	Man Without a Country.....	7		
Ollivant:	Bob, Son of Battle..........	5		
Kipling:	Jungle Books...............	6		
Warner:	Being a Boy...............	4		
Cooper:	Last of the Mohicans........	8		
Cooper:	Spy......................	5	9	
London:	Sea Wolf..................	5		
Allen:	Kentucky Cardinal..........	6		
Tarkington:	Gentleman from Indiana.....	5		
Rice:	Lovey Mary...............	5		
Porter:	Girl of the Limberlost........	7		
Montgomery	Anne of Green Gables.......	9		
Finley:	Elsie Books................	3		
Barrie:	Little Minister.............			1
Bulwer:	Last Days of Pompeii........			1
Bronte:	Jane Eyre..................			1
Churchill:	Richard Carvel.............			1
Davis:	Soldiers of Fortune..........		1	1
Dumas:	Count of Monte Christo......		1	
Ford:	Books.....................		1	
Hope:	Books.....................		1	1
Kipling:	Books.....................		1	
Kipling:	Poems....................		1	1
Longfellow:	Hiawatha..................		1	
Sienkewicz:	Quo Vadis.................		1	1
Tennyson:	Idylls of the King...........			1
	Poems....................		1	1
Thackeray:	Vanity Fair................			1
Westcott:	David Harum..............		1	1

The following table was arranged by choosing the most popular book from one list and placing it first, then by taking the one at the head of the list in the second study and placing it second, and in a corresponding manner placing the book from the third study third. Then the process was repeated for the remaining books until all had been used up.

Table III
Most Popular Books Arranged in the Order of Their Popularity
SELECTED FROM THE STUDIES OF H.C. HENDERSON, ROXANNA E. ANDERSON, FRANK O. SMITH, AND C. E. JONES.

Age 11-12

Boys	Girls
Robinson Crusoe	Little Women
Boys of '76	Uncle Tom's Cabin
Life of Washington	Robinson Crusoe
Little Men	Fairy Tales
Uncle Tom's Cabin	Little Men
Black Beauty	Under the Lilacs
Hans Andersen's Fairy Tales	Little Lord Fauntleroy
Frank on the Gunboat	Black Beauty
Gulliver's Travels	Seven Little Sisters
Longfellow's Poems	Two Little Pilgrims' Progress
Two Little Pilgrims' Progress	Life of Washington
Under the Lilacs	Life of Franklin
Hunters of the Ozarks	Little Red Riding Hood
Juan and Juanita	Eight Cousins
Lion of St. Marks	Sara Crewe
Five Little Peppers	Editha's Burglar
Frank in the Mountains	

Age 13-15

Boys	Girls
Half Back	Evangeline
Lorna Doone	Alcott
Treasure Island	Wiggin
Cooper	Man Without a Country
Motor Boys	Hans Brinker
Scott	Lorna Doone
Evangeline	Uncle Tom's Cabin
Alger Books	Spy
Kipling	Montgomery
Merchant of Venice	Bow of Orange Ribbon
Hans Brinker	Mrs. Wiggs of the Cabbage Patch
Bob, Son of Battle	Lovey Mary
Enoch Arden	Santa Claus' Partner
Alice's Adventures in Wonderland	Elsie Dinsmore
Being a Boy	Merchant of Venice
Man Without a Country	Treasure Island
Two Years Before the Mast	Birds' Christmas Carol

INTRODUCTION

Miles Standish
Whittier's Poems
Brewster's Millions

Five Little Peppers
Ivanhoe
Robinson Crusoe

Age 16-17

Boys
Parkman's Histories
Call of the Wild
Connor's Works
Julius Caesar
The Virginian
Lorna Doone
Crimson Sweater
Uncle Tom's Cabin
Clemens' Works
Half Back
Henty's Works
Dickens' Works
Midsummer Night's Dream
Churchill's Works
Little Shepherd of Kingdom Come
Hans Brinker
Ben Hur
Man Without a Country
John Halifax, Gentleman
Treasure Island

Girls
Evangeline
Dickens
Treasure Island
Julius Caesar
Little Shephard of Kingdom Come
Ivanhoe
Romeo and Juliet
Crisis
Alcott
Enoch Arden
The Virginian
Mrs. Wiggs of the Cabbage Patch
Idylls of the King
Uncle Tom's Cabin
Ramona
Lowell's Poems
Connor's Works
Hoosier Schoolmaster
Richard Carvel
Ben Hur

Among the reports which have been reviewed in this chapter there is found much divergency as to the literary quality of the choices and the proportion of so-called "serious" books chosen. In general, the form of the inquiries favors the record of "better" and more "serious" reading, and different studies differ in this.

In some matters there is substantial agreement. Both boys and girls read more fiction than anything else and like it better. In nine cases out of ten girls read more fiction than boys. Whenever this fiction has been analyzed there is a general concurrence of opinion that boys prefer fiction of adventure; that girls, particularly in the high school period, are greatly interested in sentiment and emotion, that they like, especially in the lower grades, stories about children like themselves and, in the upper grades, about people like themselves. These stories show also that girls in the high school period like novels of the day which concern manners and daily life. Girls do not like history and biography as much as do boys. During the high school years girls do like the biographies of men heroes, but they prefer those of women, and, as their ideals, prefer characters from fiction rather than those from real life.

The interest of girls in travel, adventure, and science is almost negligible.

Boys often show a real liking for history, sometimes as early as grade four. Many boys give history as a first choice. They display very little interest in books on travel or science, though more than the girls.

With increasing age preferences for juvenile fiction give way to preferences for adult fiction, and preferences for poetry increase.

Articles and Books Referred to in Chapter I

Abbott, Allen, "Reading of High School Pupils." *School Review*, 1902. X: 585-600.
Anderson R.E. "Preliminary Study of the Reading Tastes of High School Pupils." *Pedagogical Seminary*, 1912, XIX : 438-60.
Atkinson, F.W. "Reading of Young People." *Library Journal*, 1908, pp. 129-34.
Boys Reading Club (no author given). *Journal of Adolescence*, 1901, pp. 226-28.
Henderson, H.C. "Report on Child Reading." *Report of the Department of Public Instruction*, N. Y., 1897, II : 978-91.
Irving, A.P. "Home Reading of School Children." *Pedagogical Seminary*, VII : 138-40.
Jones, C.E. *Sources of Interest in English*. 1912.
Kirkpatrick, E.A., "Children's Reading." *Northwestern Monthly*, 1898,VII: 188-91; IX : 229-33.
Low, F.B., "Reading of the Modern Girl." *Nineteenth Century*, LIX:278-87.
Miner, L.B., "Voluntary Reading in English High Schools." *School Review*, XIII:180-90.

Russell, J.E., and Bullock, R.W., "Some Observations of Children's Reading." *N.E.A. Proceedings*, 1897, pp. 1015-21.
Shaw, J.C., "Children's Reading." *West Virginia Journal*, October, 1897.
Smith, F.O., "Pupils' Voluntary Reading." *Pedagoical Seminary*, 1907, XIV:208-22.
Thurber, S., "Voluntary Reading in the Classical High School." *School Review*, XIII:168-78.
True, M.B.C., "What My Children Read." *Education*, X:42-45.
Vostrovsky, C., "Children's Tastes in Reading." *Pedagogical Seminary*, VI:523-38.
Washburne, C., and Vogel, M., "The Winetka Graded Book List." American Library Association.
Wissler, C., "Interest of Children in Reading in the Elementary School." *Pedagogical Seminary*, V :523-40.

CHAPTER II
INVESTIGATIONS IN LIBRARIES

There are at least two useful methods for discovering children's preferences in books. One of these depends on the answer to questions concerning the number of books read during a certain period of time; the other, more direct in nature, propounds the question as to which book is liked best of all. In both cases there is a lack of positive proof that the children actually express their choices of books in answer to these questions.

Because of the absence of objectivity and of any other evidence except that of varying testimony, it seemed advisable in this study to observe children in their actual reading of books in a place where the opportunities for their selection were essentially the same. There is no better place for the prosecution of this idea than the public library; for here the books are identical for all and free for all. Here also we get a random sampling of children, except that the very rich rarely frequent the library, and that those present in the library may be a selection from that group intellectually more inclined. The first group is too small to warrant our attention, but the second needs further consideration.

The problem to be solved is whether this second group reads the unquestionably large amount of underground literature which is published and read. I inadvertently discovered a symptom of this type of reading while talking to a twelve-year-old boy on the East Side of New York City. This child said that he would bring me a "real book" and brought me *The $100,000 Kiss* by Nick Carter. The number of this book was 869. In other words, this author and his co-laborers had written 869 books, thousands of which had been scattered all over the country. There are others of this type; such as *Bowery Bill*, *Frank and Dick Merriwell*, and *The James Boys*, and many others which appeal to the original desire of man for quick changes, contrasts, and high intensities. The question is whether these books are read by children who do not frequent the public library or by those who do, or by both. From such cases as that mentioned above and from my own observations, the facts indicate that these books are read by both, for they feed the boys' craving for war and sport, which, expressed in a more refined way, we find represented in the former case by Tomlinson, Henty, and Altsheler, and in the latter by Barbour, Mathewson, and others. There are those, in addition, who do not desire any sort of reading but who occupy themselves with work or play or with worse. This group is not large. However, in many cases it is pathological and demands careful thought. To summarize: Indications point to the limitation of this underground reading to no particular group, but probably a large proportion of it is done by those intellectually less alert and morally more obtuse.

Eight public libraries were visited. Of these, the first six are in New York City and the other two in nearby cities. The method of procedure was as follows:

In the first place, the shelf lists of the libraries were examined and from them were listed the names of books of which there were three copies or more in the case of the smaller libraries, and four copies or more in the larger ones. With these lists in hand, the shelves were carefully inspected for three successive days and records made of books on the shelves. From these lists were subtracted (1) all books worn out, but not yet taken from the shelf list, (2) all books at the bindery, (3) all books to be mended, and (4) all books withdrawn for any other reason. Thus a live list of books was obtained. In addition, in the case of the first six libraries, a record was made of the books that were worn out, it being borne in mind that books may have formerly been popular, but, having been largely read, had lost their popularity. In this way, three columns were made: In the first column, the actual number of copies in circulation was given; in the second, the number of worn-out copies; and, in the third, the number of copies actually present on the shelves of the library.

In arranging the books in the order of popularity, the method used was to subtract the average number of copies in, multiplied by two, from the number of copies of each book and to add one for every eight copies that had been worn out. In case there were no copies of the book on the shelves, instead of subtracting, to the total number of copies was added two if that number was four or less, and three if more than four. For example:

	No. Copies.	No. Worn Out	No. In
Alcott: Little Women	18	48	0

would receive 18 points plus ⅛ of 48 plus 3—there being no copy on the shelves—27 all told. The number in should be multiplied by two because children often leave books on the shelves when they cannot get the books they want. In fact, the average case is that one in which the child, after two or three attempts to obtain a certain book, will not accept any other. This same thought suffices as a reason for adding when there are no copies of a book on the shelves. Time and time again, books not on the shelves are called for. In the face of these facts, it seemed expedient to penalize a book for having a copy left on the shelf and for rewarding it when there is none left.

As a check against the above procedure, the author remained in each library from one to three weeks observing and recording the books the children actually chose, and what books they asked for. In this manner over eight hundred observations were recorded. This method was valuable for determining the approximate ages at which books were read and whether they were read by boys or by girls. In the second place, the lists were submitted to the children's librarians in each of the libraries. Except for minor corrections, in each case the results were corroborated by the evidence of the librarians.

Library No. 1 is situated in the heart of the Ghetto. Here, concentrated in a small area, are peoples gathered from many lands. This particular library is frequented largely by Jews, the majority of whom come from Russia. Among these people, the struggle for existence is very severe. That they need help is evidenced by ninety-eight public or charitable organizations within a space of thirty blocks. In the afternoon when the papers are out, one rushes up to get the latest news and finds that the newspaper is printed in a foreign tongue—Yiddish. It gives one the impression of being in a foreign country; foreign dishes in the restaurant, foreign signs on the windows. In the heart of these surroundings is the playground, bandstand, one or two charitable organizations, the public school, and Library No. 1. The author visited this library daily for more than three weeks, getting acquainted with the children, talking with them about their reading, talking with the librarian concerning the children's preferences for books, and what was most prolific of results—slipping around and looking over the shoulders of children deeply interested in their books.

The more formal method of tabulating the actual number of books in circulation has been mentioned. Evidence of a book's popularity not so quantitative but none the less important will now be considered.

Alcott may be cited as an example for the girls.

1. There are 115 copies of Alcott on the active list while 377 copies have been worn out. No other series of books approaches this record.

2. The card catalog is black where the lists of Alcott's books are. Having read one book the girls hunt carefully to find out what others have been written and thus blacken the cards.

3. The average number of copies on the shelves was 30, but these in part were returned the afternoon before.

4. There were many inquiries for Alcott when I was present in the room. I also observed many children reading Alcott.

Altsheler is the most popular author for boys of this age.

1. The number of copies in the library is 57. The average number of copies on the shelves for three days was 3.3

2. The number of copies worn out was 238, although the series is comparatively modern.

3. The card catalog is positively black where the cards for these books are located.

4. Out of thirty-nine observations of the choices of books from those just recently placed on the shelves was first choice in 28. The boys stood in line for from fifteen to sixty minutes waiting for an Altsheler and would have nothing else. I have seen them turn away disgusted because there was no copy of this author present. After witnessing the boys scramble and struggle for these books, no one doubts that Altsheler is the most interesting writer for these boys.

Henty comes second with boys.

1. The number of copies in this library is 21. The average number of copies on the shelves for three days was 4.

2. The number of copies worn out is 348.

3. The blackness of the card catalog ranked as "3" if Altsheler was "1."

4. Henty was first choice for four times when the children chose from books recently replaced on the shelves. In

addition, the children read Henty in the room very frequently, and having taken me for an inspector asked for "fifty Altshelers and some Hentys."

Barbour is also a favorite author.

1. The number of copies in the library was 29. The average number of copies on the shelves was 2.
2. The number of copies worn out was 28.
3. The blackness of the card catalog was ranked as "3."
4. For three times the most popular book with boys in the choosing of juvenile fiction was Barbour. Children asked for Barbour and were observed reading him only less often than Altsheler and Henty.

The same type of evidence places Clemens very near the front in popularity.

The scores were obtained in all cases (1) by evaluating the number of books, the number worn out, the number in, and the number out (for details, see page 16); (2) by adding to the number obtained by the above method three times the number of times children were observed reading particular books; and (3) by adding to the sum obtained in methods (1) and (2) a number representing the judgment of the librarians. Thus there was obtained a composite score of these three methods which in the particular library is as reliable an indication of the relative popularity of these books as could be obtained under the complex conditions under which the study was carried on. The scores in every case were so weighted as to represent most nearly the actual facts. For example, the opinion of a librarian who had been in a particular library for some years was given more weight than that of a librarian who had not been there sufficiently long to become thoroughly acquainted with the books. And, finally, the results are largely dependent upon the author's own observations for more than three months during which time he mingled with the children of the various libraries, read their books, tabulated the books they had withdrawn, observed their readings, and sought as far as possible to get their point of view. The tables following are summaries of the information gained by this investigation.

The Interests of Boys

The interests of boys from 10½ to 13½ years take three definite paths: (1) war and scouting, (2) school and sports, and (3) adventure of a more peaceful sort in the great out-of-doors, best exemplified by the Boy Scouts. In each case there must be actual heroes. A boy prefers living characters. He will leave history however well written for a story of historical nature.

The premier writer of the first type, Altsheler, makes one think the thoughts of his heroes. In the *Guns of Bull Run*, the Southern heroes talk for a brief space and we feel immediately in sympathy with them for they are brave, honorable, and true. But soon we are transferred to the Union camp. Here again there is found courage, honesty, strength of muscle, daring, courtesy, and honor in the cousins of the Southern heroes. War consists in charges, daredevil rides, hair-breadth escapes, and jolly good friendships. The horror, death, agony, the grind of training are rarely mentioned, and, when they are, are hurriedly passed over. Let us look more minutely at the *Scouts of the Valley*. In the frontispiece, we have a picture of a gloomy forest, a wounded man fighting for loved ones, women and children frightened, bedraggled and downcast. The hero is strong in muscle and accurate of movement, for he can "bring the paddle into the boat, grasp the rifle, and carry it to his shoulder with a single continuous movement." The hero was born and bred in the forest. "He was the great picture of fact, not of fancy, a human being animated by a living dauntless soul." This hero is unafraid, although in constant danger. He is constantly fighting the Indians, yet bears them no hatred. On the

TABLE IV
TYPES OF FICTION MOST INTERESTING TO BOYS
MATERIAL COLLECTED FROM LIBRARIES IN AND NEAR NEW YORK CITY

Represents (*a*) the points obtained by each of the most popular authors of fiction in each library, (*b*) the total points for each author. Points obtained by evaluating (1) the number of books, the number worn out, the number in and the number out, (2) the number of observations, and (3) the judgments of the librarians. Details of method on page 16

Author	Library Circulation (typical) per month	No. 1 11,385	No. 2 4,127	No. 3 12,624	No. 4 6,537	No. 5 16,337	No. 6 6,138	No. 7 2,586	No. 8 9,237	Total
Altsheler:	War and Scouting	257	62	160	242	373	42	..	65	1201
Barbour:	School and Sports	79	48	140	59	237	39	22	65	689
Tomlinson:	War and Scouting	50	7	47	20	158	28	11	46	367
Burton:	Boy Scouts	..	9	46	30	67	22	..	78	252
Clemens:	Strenuous Adventure	74	22	..	20	64	9	14	33	236
Henty:	War and Scouting	127	6	47	..	..	8	..	4	192
Dudley:	School and Sports	..	..	18	18	127	..	..	..	163
Munroe:	War, School, and Sports	..	..	40	19	22	17	7	20	125
Heyliger:	Boy Scouts	20	9	21	16	48	..	5	..	119
Quirk:	*Freshman Eight* (School and Sports)	..	6	20	10	21	14	8	20	99
Mathewson:	School and Baseball	..	10	17	10	21	8	..	20	86
Eaton:	Boy Scouts	20	..	21	..	..	6	..	33	80
Stevenson:	Railroad Adventure	..	..	..	27	42	..	..	10	79
Doyle:	Strenuous Adventure	20	..	..	..	20	13	..	18	71
Malone:	West Point Series	..	..	..	28	29	6	8	..	71

Author	Title/Description									Total
Otis:	Strenuous Adventure (*Toby Tyler*)	28	.	.	.	19	5	.	18	70
Stevenson:	War, Piracy, and Scouting	30	6	.	9	.	8	4	11	68
McNeil:	War and Scouting	.	.	.	.	45	14	.	.	59
Fennemore:	Boy Scouts	.	.	.	28	29	.	.	.	57
Grinnell:	Outdoor Life with boat, trap, and gun	.	.	.	.	26	6	.	18	50
Camp:	School and Sports	.	.	.	.	49	.	.	.	49
Elderdice:	T.H.Hicks Series, School and Sports	.	.	10	.	38	.	.	.	48
Burgess:	Boy Scouts	.	.	.	16	30	.	.	.	46
Sabin:	Scouting and War (*Buffalo Bill*)	.	5	13	.	17	.	.	8	43
Williams:	School and Sports	.	.	.	.	41	.	.	.	41
Paine:	School and Sports (*Sandy Sawyer, Sophomore*)	.	.	8	10	20	.	.	.	38
True:	War and Scouting	.	.	.	.	16	.	.	18	34
French:	Sport	.	.	.	.	17	.	.	9	26
Doubleday:	*Cattle Ranch to College* (School and Sports)	12	.	12	.	.	.	.	.	24
Wyss:	*Swiss Family Robinson* (Adventure)	10	.	.	.	9	.	.	4	23
Fisher:	School and Sports	.	.	9	9	.	.	.	.	20... (20)
Gregor:	*White Otter* (Adventure)	.	.	9	.	20	.	.	11	20
Hale:	*Man Without a Country* (Adventure)	20	.	.	.	.	.	.	.	20
Garland:	Adventure (*Ross Grant Tenderfoot*)	.	.	10	9	.	.	.	.	19
Pier:	School and Sports	.	.	.	.	15	.	.	4	19
Holland:	Boy Scouts	.	.	.	8	.	.	.	9	17
Hobson:	School and Sports (*Buck Jones at Annapolis*)	.	.	.	16	.	.	.	.	16
Johnson:	*Williams at West Point* (School and Sports)	.	5	.	8	.	.	.	.	13

	Library	No. 1	No. 2	No. 3	No. 4	No. 5	No. 6	No. 7	No. 8	
Dumas:	*War and Strenuous Adventure*.	14								14
Hugo:	*Les Misérables* (Adventure)									12
Hughes:	*School and Sports*.	12								12
Kutz:	*School and Sports*.						12			12
Hendry:	*Connie Morgan in Alaska* (Adventure)								11	11
Kipling:	*Jungle Books* (Adventure)		10							10
Dickens:	*Oliver Twist* (Adventure)		10							10
Scott:	*Ivanhoe* (War and Adventure)		10							10
Hawkes:	*King of the Thundering Herd* (Adventure)							10		10
DeFoe:	*Robinson Crusoe* (Adventure)				4			5		9
Dodge:	*Hans Brinker* (Adventure)					9				9
Canfield:	*Boys of Rincorn Ranch* (Adventure)						8			8
Eldred:	*Oak Street Boys' Club* (Adventure)						8			8
Dimock:	*Boy Scouts* (*Be Prepared*)								8	8

Percentages below calculated from the actual number of books and not from the number of authors.

Library	No. 1	No. 2	No. 3	No. 4	No. 5	No. 6	No. 7	No. 8	Average	Median
War and Scouting	43	29	24	25	30	40	28	32	32	29.5
School and Sports	17	29	38	32	42	20	32	20	29	30.5
Boy Scouts	16	19	14	18	10	17	16	20	16	16.5
Strenuous Adventure	24	23	24	25	18	21	24	28	23	23.5
Total	100	100	100	100	100	100	100	100	100	100.

contrary, he rather admires their "powerful muscles" and sympathizes with their longing for the freedom of the great out-of-doors. In this book there are four other white men who accompany the leader. They find the Indians on the point of rising up against the whites and must need investigate further. All are captured except the hero, who, by craftily laid plans and unexcelled courage, succeeds in freeing one after another of his comrades until he has the Indians so mystified that they attribute these liberations to the "evil spirit." The author gives a vivid account of the Indian chief's council at which plans against the whites were being concocted. The hero, by creeping silently upon them, protected by the dark night and by the absence of dogs, the Indians having left these unnecessary animals at home, learns of their plans. Armed with these facts, he warns the settlers, helps to protect the women and children, receives the plaudits of his superiors, is captured and afterwards released by an admiring Indian, and in general comes out victor. The leading character of the book acts so nobly that the chief of the Wyandottes will not let him be killed and when a blood-thirsty woman is about to split the prisoner's head with her tomahawk, the chief slits the captive's thongs and he escapes to the forest.

Consider the titles of some of this author's books: *Sword of Antietam*, *Scouts of the Valley*, *Lone Star*, *Rock of Chickamauga*, *On the Plains with Custer*. In all of these there is the same appeal of adventure, of battle, and of victory. There is no halfway point. The victory is clean cut and decisive. Not so exciting, yet just as warlike are the works of Henty. *By Pike and Dyke*, *By England's Aid*, *With Wolf in Canada*, *With Lee in Virginia* are illustrative titles by this author.

The second large division centers around the school. Barbour is a representative author of this type. His heroes excel in baseball, football, and in other sports. They are jolly good fellows, are honorable, and attentive to their lessons. In the story of *The Half-Back*, a young man arrives from the country at a fashionable but rather rigorous boarding school. He has breathed the air of the country and has acquired a rugged constitution. Having played on the eighth grade team at home, he surprises his comrades with his ability to punt. By accident he saves the life of a boy who is thus brought to know and admire the hero of the story. The former is very wealthy, while the latter is very poor; yet their friendship is very close. One follows the hero breathlessly from escapade to escapade in his successful school career. He makes the football team and finds the coach a man after his own liking. Throughout his busy life, however, he finds time to write long chatty letters to his mother. Later on he saves a boy from drowning and again comes to the focus of attention. Fill in imaginatively the details of this sketch: There are two minutes to play; it is the third down and ten to go with the score a tie, a wide sweeping end run places the ball in front of the goal, and the hero with one well directed kick sends the ball squarely between the uprights just as the referee's whistle announces the end of the game. For the man who has made such a kick, nothing is good enough. He is carried off the field on the shoulders of his shouting comrades and the game is over—and you have the type of book that Barbour writes and that the boys read. Here are some of the titles: *Weatherby's Inning*, *Hitting the Line*, *Left-Tackle Thayer*, and *Four in Camp*.

The third large division of boys' interests concerns itself with the Boy Scouts. The grip that this movement has on the boys is illustrated by the number of popular books which center around the Boy Scout movement. A good example of this type is Heyliger's *Don Strong of the Wolf Patrol*. The hero, Don Strong, at the beginning of the story is a rather

TABLE V

MOST POPULAR BOOKS OF NON-FICTION AND OF WAR. BOYS

RESULTS OBTAINED FROM EIGHT PUBLIC LIBRARIES IN AND AROUND NEW YORK CITY

Points deduced as in "Fiction" are the sum of those obtained by the methods mentioned below. The points were evaluated from (1) the number of copies possessed by the library, the number worn out, the number on the shelves, and the number out; (2) multiplying by three the number of times each book was observed being read, and, (3) the judgments of librarians. Details of method on page 16

Library Circulation (typical) per month	No. 1 11,385	No. 2 4,127	No. 3 12,624	No. 4 6,537	No. 5 16,337	No. 6 6,138	No. 7 2,586	No. 8 9,237	Total
Boy Scout Official Handbook, Signal Code....	14	7	18	7	24	9	12	12	103
About Lincoln (Nicolay, Cravens, Moore, Baldwin)..................	..	4	23	..	19	8	4	4	62
Collins: Boy's First and Second Books of Model Aeroplanes........	..	6	13	..	8	8	9	14	58
Du Chaillu: In African Forest and Jungle...	..	..	..	..	47	..	8	..	55
Baldwin: Old Stories of the East........	24	..	..	..	16	..	..	..	40
Harper's: Handy Book for Boys, Camping, Scouting and Electricity...	..	6	..	5	12	..	5	6	34

										Total
Life of Washington	(Brooks, Hill)	: :	: :	: :	: :	19	:	4	4	27
Beard:	American Boys Handy Book	: :	: :	5	: :	6	7	:	5	23
	Harpers Outdoor Book for Boys, and Indoor Book	: :	: :	15	: :	: :	7	:	:	22
Cody:	Adventures of Buffalo Bill	: :	6	10	: :	: :	:	:	5	21
Stockton:	Buccaneers and Pirates of Our Coast	: :	6	: :	: :	: :	:	:	:	21
Shaw:	Discoverers and Explorers	21	: :	: :	: :	16	:	:	5	21
Gordy:	American Leaders and Heroes	: :	: :	: :	4	12	:	4	:	20
Bolton:	Discoverers and Explorers	: :	: :	: :	: :	12	:	:	6	18
Bass:	Stories of Pioneer Life	16	: :	: :	: :	: :	:	:	4	16
Books on Magic:		: :	: :	: :	: :	: :	:	:	:	16
Cutler:	Conundrums	11	: :	: :	: :	12	:	:	:	16
Eggleston:	Story of American Life and Adventure	: :	: :	: :	: :	5	:	:	:	15
Tappan:	Makers of Many Things	14	: :	: :	: :	10	5	:	:	15
Faris:	Makers of our History	12	: :	: :	: :	: :	:	:	:	14
Gordy:	Colonial Days	: :	5	7	: :	: :	:	:	:	12
Moffett:	Careers of Danger and Daring	11	: :	: :	: :	: :	:	:	:	12
Moore:	Pilgrims and Puritans	11	: :	: :	: :	: :	:	:	:	11
Guerber:	Story of the 13 Colonies	11	: :	: :	: :	: :	:	:	:	11
Cable:	Famous Adventures and Prison Escapes of the Civil War	: :	: :	: :	: :	: :	:	:	:	11
Hill:	On the Trail of Grant and Lee	: :	: :	10	: :	: :	:	:	:	10
Eastman:	Indian Stories	: :	: :	10	: :	: :	:	:	:	10
Tappan:	When Knights Were Bold	: :	: :	10	: :	: :	:	:	:	10
Soley:	Boys of 1812	: :	: :	9	: :	: :	:	:	:	9
Eggleston:	Stories of Great Americans for Little Americans	: :	: :	9	: :	: :	:	:	:	9
Arnold:	Story of Ancient People	9	: :	: :	: :	: :	:	:	:	9
		9	: :	: :	: :	: :	:	:	:	9

Marshall:	Island Story	.	.	.	.	8
Johnston:	Leading American Soldiers	.	.	.	.	8
Cooke:	Stories of France	.	.	.	.	8
Physioc:	Manual for Boy Scouts	.	.	8	.	8
Dalton:	How to Swim	.	.	8	.	8
Hill:	Fighting a Fire	.	8	.	.	8
Brooks:	True Story of Christopher Columbus	.	.	.	.	7
Southwork and Paine:	Bugle Calls of Liberty	.	.	.	.	7

War Books

(Very popular with boys in all libraries, but too recent to obtain any comparative evaluation of their popularity.)

Empey: Over the Top, First Call
Hay: First 100,000
O'Brien: Outwitting the Hun
Knyvett: Over There with the Australians
Hall: High Adventure: Kitchener's Mob
Middleton: Glorious Exploits of the Air
Paine: Fighting Fleets
Brown: The A. E. F.
Buswell: Ambulance No. 10
Huard: My Home in the Field of Mercy; My Home in the Field of Honor
Braucker: Cavalry of the Clouds

careless, good-natured, poor lad with scarcely an interest outside the petty rounds of his school and a few friends. His father, a carpenter, would ask him over and over again for help, but the son would not stick at a job for any length of time. However, through the instrumentality of a big-hearted scoutmaster, he becomes mildly interested, then wholly interested in scouting. He must now be kind to someone each day, and must earn some money before he can become even a second class scout. Don finds both of these demands peculiarly difficult because of his inherent inability for continuity of effort and because of a friend who scorns the whole business. But he was directed to the building of a bird's house, made a success of it, so much so that he earned sufficient money to attend high school the following year. Through hikes into the great out-of-doors, the building and tagging of huts, the impetus towards clean living and fair dealing was truly marvelous. Through it all, he had the coöperation of his kind-hearted father and an intelligent sister. This book shows clearly the attitude of the boy himself towards the Boy Scouts, and the fact that the boys read it and like it is one of the most hopeful signs found among the results of this investigation.

When non-fiction is considered, only in rare cases is there found any steady interest at this age. Many books which are popular utilize the love for adventure. Boys read the what-and-how-to-do books with the exception of those on cooking, and most of the biography and history, while the girls read the literature and the plays. In biography and history, it is worthy of note that the popular books are those which give their account as nearly as possible in story form—*Stories of Pioneer Life*, *A Story of Great Americans for Little Americans*, *The Island Story*. Even these must be about war and adventure. The interest of the boys in *Popular Mechanics* and *Scientific American* is noteworthy.

The Interests of Girls

Between the ages of 10½ and 13½, the sex difference in the interest in reading is most marked. Girls and boys read, almost entirely, different books. It is difficult to imagine a strong, healthy American boy of twelve years reading *Little Women*, and almost as difficult to imagine his sister of the same age reading an Altsheler, although the latter does happen at times. The girl does not care much for hairbreadth escapes from bullets and tomahawks. If there are to be adventures and escapes, they must needs be for punishment for the infraction of some school rule. In nearly every case, a book, to be popular, must tell of boys and girls poor but respectable and usually proud, who hide their poverty the best they can and in every case keep their honor unsullied and their minds clean. These young people even in their poverty are forgetful of self, and help others on all occasions, spreading sunshine wherever they go. Usually they are very conscious of their lack of elegant clothes. The girls feel most keenly the contrast between cheap muslins and rich silks. Gradually the prospect brightens, for usually through the efforts of the heroines, but always in some way or other, money comes into the family coffers. The kind mother can have a new dress; all the girls are able to buy new clothes; the mortgage is paid off; and virtue gets its reward. If there is a love story, few clouds darken the horizon. If these conditions are met, the book is a "perfectly splendid" one and has a "perfectly splendid ending."

There are four kinds of fiction which are of especial interest to girls of this age: (1) stories of home life, (2) stories of school life, (3) fairy stories, (4) love stories. As an example of the first type, let us consider *Little Women*, the most popular book for girls that was ever written.

The story opens upon a good, respectable, and cultivated family who are poor. The mother is one of those sympathetic persons who understands girls, for she combines within herself kindness, sympathy, and love. Her daughters love her dearly. She teaches them the gentle dignity and refinement of Christian ideals and her teaching is not lost upon the girls. Kindliness to others is the first principle of this household. Even on Christmas morning, all of them take their breakfast to a poverty-stricken family. This kind act, however, does not pass unseen, and the rich neighbor next door sends them a wonderful Christmas supper. Two of the young ladies are invited to a pretty dance at which one of them sprains her ankle and is escorted home by a young man, nephew and only relative of the rich neighbor next door. This is the beginning of a close friendship between the two families, giving an opening for the obtaining of money so necessary for our heroines' happiness. The nephew falls in love with one girl and is refused, but finally marries her sister and "they live happily ever after." The girls have many temptations but overcome them all; and many burdens, but bear them all. They have their reward in their host of friends, in the gentle happiness which comes of true love, in openness of character and in sympathy.

Laura E. Richards' *Peggy* is an excellent example of the interest in stories of school life. The spirit of this, compared with the book just mentioned above, is far more modern. The eternal feminine, however, is just as evident. Peggy alights from the train into the midst of a group of boarding school girls, among whom, though she is homesick for the country and for the simple joys of family affection, she makes friends. She sees very soon that her wardrobe is slim in comparison with that of some of the other girls and, above all, out of style. Her uncle, however, sends her a large box of many things necessary to full enjoyment of school life and by this means her room is made comfortable. Peggy wins friends through her open disposition and gains admiration because of physical strength which rapidly develops in the gymnasium and in basketball. Things run along smoothly until she meets a wild nature, the "scapegoat" who is "D.D. and D.—dear, delightful and dangerous." This bright, artistic, but uncurbed individual leads our "innocent" into many a scrape until Peggy finds that she herself is thoroughly trusted by the principal of the school. She then changes her ways and becomes loyal to the school, to her teachers, stands by her friends, and even runs off a man who is attempting to steal the jewelry of the girls. Marshmallow toasts, school dramatics, and studies follow each other with kaleidoscopic rapidity. Above all, friendships strong and true are formed and love is in many places.

The third interest of girls is in fairy stories. Although these stories are generally omitted from this study, it seemed best to include *Alice's Adventures in Wonderland*, which is generally familiar and needs no mention here.

The last mentioned type of book which is interesting to girls is the love story. Of these Woolsey's *In the High Valley* is a good illustration. The scene opens in England where a brother and sister and their mother live in a small country home. The young man feels that he must come to America to make his way in the world. They meet some American girls who are "horribly" non-English and who are, for some unaccountable reason, proud of the fact that they are Americans. After the customary leave-takings, brother and sister are off on their journey and soon land in New York City. They are thoroughly mystified at its hospitality, its extravagance, and at many other of its characteristics. Soon, however, they are moving into "The High Valley in Colorado." Here are a few delightful, cultivated American people, who attempt to make the English girl feel at home and from whom she holds aloof for some reason or other. Her actions are English and queer; those of the American women are wholesouled, efficient, generous, and kind, but they care little for formalities while the English girl is almost the reverse. The latter falls sick and is nursed so carefully

TABLE VI
TYPES OF FICTION MOST INTERESTING TO GIRLS
Material collected from libraries in and near New York City

Represents (a) the points obtained by each of the most popular authors of fiction in each library, (b) the total points for each author. Points obtained by evaluating; (1) the number of books, the number worn out, the number in and the number out; (2) the number of observations; and (3) the judgment of the librarians. Details of method on page 16

Library Circulation (typical) per month	No. 1 11,385	No. 2 4,127	No. 3 12,624	No. 4 6,537	No. 5 16,337	No. 6 6,138	No. 7 2,586	No. 8 9,237	Total
Alcott: Series of Home Life and Mild Adventure	132	41	107	44	68	32	25	89	538
Richards: School Stories and Home (*Peggy*)	36	5	54	32	34	23	5	23	212
Wiggin: Home and School: *Rebecca of Sunnybrook Farm*	37	6	30	16	68	13	18	21	209
Burnett: Stories of Unusual Kindliness and Usefulness	81	..	31	16	31	11	16	..	186
Sidney: Home and Neighborhood (Little Pepper Series)	18	12	37	16	78	17	6	..	184
Woolsey: Home Life and Mild Adventure (*In the High Valley*)	37	9	49	34	29	6	..	9	173
Deland: Home Life and Mild Adventure (*Katrina*)	37	..	53	10	37	12	..	10	159
Montgomery: Home and School (*Anne of Green Gables*)	32	3	..	..	38	11	12	23	119

Author	Title									Total
Rankin:	Home and Neighborhood (*Adopting of Rosa Marie*)	∶	10	11	16	37	12	∶	6	92
Taggart:	Home, Mild Adventure (*LittleGrey House*)	∶	9	9	9	36	∶	3	26	92
Vaile:	School and Home (*Orcutt Girls*)	37	6	32	22	26	∶	∶	∶	86
Dodgson:	Semi-Fairy Tales (*Alice's Adventures, etc.*)	31	∶	11	∶	27	9	∶	7	85
Jacobs:	Home and School (*Joan's Jolly Vacation*)	∶	∶	8	10	32	14	∶	10	74
Dix:	Historical Background (*Merrylips*)	∶	∶	∶	8	30	11	2	8	69
Knipe:	Historical Background, Home (*Maid of Old Manhattan*)	32	8	17	∶	∶	6	4	∶	67
Porter:	*Pollyanna*	∶	3	∶	10	38	11	∶	∶	62
Phelps:	School and Home (*Gypsy's Year at the Golden Crescent*)	∶	∶	10	∶	30	10	∶	9	59
Clarke:	Home and Neighborhood (*Dotty Dimple Series*)	∶	∶	∶	∶	37	6	∶	∶	51
Du Bois:	School and Adventure (*Lass of the Silver Sword*)	∶	∶	10	8	19	∶	7	7	49
Brown:	Secret of the Clan (*Lonesomest Doll*)	10	∶	11	6	∶	∶	7	7	48
Dodge:	Home and Community (*Hans Brinker*)	10	∶	10	16	26	∶	4	∶	46
Webster:	School and College (*When Patty Went to College*)	26	3	∶	10	∶	11	2	∶	42
Ray:	Home and School (*Teddy, Her Profession*)	∶	∶	∶	8	20	∶	∶	∶	39
Ruskin:	*King of the Golden River*	11	∶	∶	7	21	5	∶	∶	38
Spyri:	Home and Relations (*Heidi*)	∶	5	11	∶	∶	∶	4	5	37
Craik:	*Little Lame Prince, John Halifax*	12	5	10	7	∶	∶	∶	∶	27
Stowe:	*Uncle Tom's Cabin*	12	4	9	∶	∶	∶	∶	∶	25

Author	Book									Total
Jackson:	Home and Neighborhood (*Nelly's Silber Mine*)	6	9	:	:	:	:	:	10	25
Brown:	*Her 16th Year*, *Two College Girls*	:	:	:	:	:	:	:	20	20
Rice:	Home and Neighborhood (*Mrs. Wiggs of the Cabbage Patch*)....18	:	10	:	8	:	:	:	:	18
Pyle:	*Christmas Angel*, *Counterpane Fairy*	:	:	8	:	:	:	:	18	18
Curtis:	Stories with Historical Background	:	:	:	:	:	:	18	:	18
Smith:	School (*Peggy Raymond's School Days*)	:	:	16	:	:	:	:	:	16
Seaman:	Home and Neighborhood (*Boarded up House*)	9	:	:	:	:	:	5	:	14
Dickens:	Historical Background (*Tale of Two Cities*)....8	4	:	:	:	2	:	:	:	14
Cummins:	Unusual Pathos (*Lamplighter*)....13	:	:	:	:	:	:	:	:	1?
Gerson:	*A Modern Esther*....12	:	:	6	:	:	:	:	:	1
Jamison:	Home and Adventure (*Lady Jane*)	6	:	:	:	:	:	:	11	1
Ashenum:	School (*Isabel Carlton's Year*)	:	:	:	:	:	:	:	:	1
Singmaster:	Home and School (*When Sarah Saved the Day*)	:	:	:	:	:	10	:	:	1
Martin:	Home and School (*Emmy Lou*)	:	10	:	:	:	:	:	:	1
Haskell:	*Katrinka*, Russian Story	:	7	:	:	1	:	:	:	1
Sewell:	Kindness to Animals (*Black Beauty*)	:	:	:	:	3	:	5	:	5

The percentages calculated below were calculated from the total number of books liked, and not from authors mentioned above.

Home....................................37
Home and School....................19
School..................................15
Love.....................................7
Fairy Stories..........................6
Historical Background.............6
Miscellaneous......................10

by the American neighbors that she capitulates entirely. A hard student of electrical engineering and his sister, who is also the sister of one of the American women of the community, visit the neighborhood. The electrical engineer falls in love with the English girl and the English boy with the American girl and thus a double engagement is announced.

Girls have a distressingly small interest in non-fiction. They read and act out a few plays and read a small bit of literature. For the most part, they seem to care but little for the rush of events, reading few magazines which concern themselves about such things. *St. Nicholas*, of course, is read, but chiefly for its stories.

SUMMARY

In conclusion, the foregoing data indicate:

1. That the interests of boys and girls in reading are very dissimilar.

2. That the major interests in reading of boys from 10 to 13 years include four general types of fiction: (*a*) Books concerned with war and scouting; (*b*) those concerned with school and sports; (*c*) those concerned with the Boy Scouts; and (*d*) those concerned with strenuous adventure. Books concerned with war and scouting include 32 per cent of the total books of fiction. Books concerned with school and sports, 29 per cent; books on Boy Scouts, 16 per cent; books of strenuous adventure, 23 per cent.

3. That Altsheler, a writer of war and scouting, is the most popular writer for boys in the libraries examined; that the boys stand in line in some libraries for an hour or more in order to get a book by this author; that he is almost twice as popular as any other author.

4. That Barbour is the most popular writer of school and sports; Burton of Boy Scouts; and Clemens of strenuous adventure.

5. That in an analysis of these books, it is found that the popular writers appeal most often to the instincts of mastery,

fighting, love of sensory life for its own sake, original attention, and approval and scornful behavior.

6. That in non-fiction, the interest centers around what-and-how-to-do books. The *Boy Scout Manual* is by far the most popular of this group, although books on aeroplanes, submarines, kites, engines, puzzles and magic are in certain seasons much sought after.

7. That the interest in biography and history is confined to those authors who can write history and biography in the form of an exciting story.

8. That *St. Nicholas, Popular Mechanics, Scientific American, American Boy,* and *Boys' Life* are the most popular magazines among the boys.

9. That the interests of girls are principally concerned with fiction which portrays: (*a*) home, 37 per cent; (*b*) home and school, 19 per cent; (*c*) school, 15 per cent; (*d*) fairy stories, 6 per cent; (*e*) stories with historical background, 6 per cent; (*f*) love, 7 per cent, and (*g*) miscellaneous, 10 per cent.

10. That Alcott, whose books are largely concerned with home life, is far more popular with girls in these eight libraries than is any other author; that Wiggin and Sidney should also be noted in this group concerned with home life; Richards leads in the home and school group; Dodgson in the fairy tales; Knipe in stories with a historical background; and Woolsey in love stories.

11. That those authors popular with girls appeal largely to the following instincts: maternal, kindliness, attention to others, response to approval and scornful behavior, and, to a less degree than in the case of boys, to rivalry.

12. That except for a few books on cooking, crocheting, dramatics and poetry, girls fail to show interest in non-fiction.

13. That *St. Nicholas* is the only magazine liked to any extent by girls and that, in general, tables of magazines are largely patronized by boys.

CHAPTER III
RESULTS OF THE QUESTIONNAIRE

In another place[1] the author has set forth the answers given by children to questions asking directly why they liked certain books. Many of these answers seemed so stilted and formal that it was impossible to judge whether they were the real reasons or not. It seems evident therefore, that children, even those of high school age, have not the ability to explain why they like certain books rather than others. On the other hand, the facts indicate that it is entirely feasible to obtain from children approximately correct responses in regard to their choices of books, provided the questions are simple enough. If a child could know that the answers obtained would under no occasion be used against him, the chances that the responses would be correct are increased; if he had only a few simple, direct questions put to him orally, his attention would be concentrated on the task at hand and the responses would be more accurate; and, finally, if the children wrote only their first names, their identity thereby being hidden, they would more freely attack the task at hand. Thus the two conditioning elements, the situation and the question of 'drive,' are provided for—the answers, of course, being not only determined by the simplicity of the situation, "What book do I like?" as proposed by the experimenter, but also by the subject's inner condition as exemplified by such questions as, "Is it worth while?" "Can I afford to write down the name of the book that actually thrills me?" "What would the teacher think if he knew?" and "What would Mary think?" etc.

[1] *Children's Interests in Reading.* Teachers College Contributions to Education, No. 107.

The following questions, based on the criteria of simplicity, brevity, and accuracy, were submitted either in person or by a friendly principal to the schools of Fayetteville, Arkansas; Lawrence, Kansas; Stuttgart, Arkansas; and Washington, D. C. In all, responses from 3,598 pupils were obtained. In only rare cases were there no responses from individual pupils. A brief statement of the purpose of the study was given to the pupils, and a conscious attempt made on the part of the examiner to put himself *en rapport* with them. Next, the fact was emphasized that the school authorities would not see the answers of the individual student, and a plea to the students for actual truth was made. As an aid in helping pupils lose their identity they were asked to write their first names only. Other items asked for were age and grade or year. The questions used in each case were:

I. 1. Will you kindly write down for me the name of the book you like best of all the books you have ever read?
   2. Will you write down for me the name of the book you like next best of all the books you have ever read?
   3. Will you write down the book you like next best and next best of all the books you have ever read until you have written five books arranged in the order of your preference?

II. 1. Will you write down for me the name of the magazine you like best of all the magazines you have ever read?
   2. Will you write down the name of the magazine you like next best of all the magazines you have ever read?
   3. Will you write down the name of the magazine you like next best of all the magazines you have ever read so that altogether you have written three magazines, arranged in the order of your preference?

The children took up the business of writing the answers earnestly and in many cases eagerly. There were those who made play of the performance, but they were few. In several cases the principal accompanying me said that he was certain that the pupils were doing their best to answer the questions as accurately as they could. Those who took the matter as a joke could be easily detected in the unusual character of their answers, such as the nineteen-year-old senior asserting *Mother Goose* was her favorite book. These chance errors which crept in were insufficient to cause any deviation from the central tendency of interests. The material thus secured from the students was gone through for the purpose of selecting a list of books and magazines which were more often chosen than any others. Each of these books and magazines was given a number by means of which it was subsequently identified. All the replies of the students were then tabulated, each book or magazine being registered either by a letter which designated its general type, for example, fiction, or by the number which identified both the book and its class. In this manner each book on the popular list received a number of votes and each type of book likewise received its quota. The summary tables include all books or magazines from both the popular and the non-popular groups.

The first town studied was Fayetteville, Arkansas. This town, which is the seat of the state university, is situated in the Ozark Mountains and has a population of approximately 6,000. The pupils questioned extended from the sixth grade through the high school. Their favorite books were so tabulated as to indicate year by year the number of times each was chosen. In the second place all the books were classified into adult fiction, juvenile fiction, adventure, biography, history, poetry, science, travel, information, humor, miscellaneous. Record was also kept of the cases where no choice was stated. Lists of books most often chosen were made. All conclusions concerning types of books found interesting were drawn from their concrete reports of particular books. All magazines were classified as follows: adult fiction, juvenile fiction, adventure, nature, pictures, woman's arts, science, current events, humor, and miscellaneous. Record was kept of the cases where no choice was stated. Lists of magazines most often chosen were made. The magazines listed in this study as *popular* include approximately 90 per cent of all the choices, while the books listed as *popular* include very nearly 45 per cent of all the choices.

The next town to be studied was Lawrence, Kansas. This town of about 12,000 inhabitants is also the seat of a state university. Exactly the same questions were asked the pupils, under conditions as nearly the same as it was possible to make them, and the replies, 733 in all, were classified and tabulated exactly as in the first town.

The third study was made at Washington, D. C. The principal of the New Central High School was kind enough to give to the pupils of his high school the same questions used on the two previous occasions. All the children here are from the high school, while in the other two studies there are some from the sixth, seventh, and eighth grades. There are 1,879 returns in all, a number large enough to minimize the effect of whatever chance errors might arise. The same system of classification and the same methods of tabulation were used as in the other studies.

The last town to be investigated for the purpose of finding children's interests in reading was Stuttgart, a small town located in Arkansas. The principal coöperated in the undertaking to such an extent that the author was able to use this community to find the relation between results obtained with successive reactions to the same questions. Thus the questions were submitted to the pupils of that town six

Results of the Questionnaire 33

months and five days apart, in the fall and again in the following spring. Only the choices of pupils appearing in both tests—200 in all—were tabulated. By means of this procedure an attempt was made to determine (1) the number of times the same book would be placed a second time in the identical position by the same individual; (2) the number of times the same individual would rechoose a book but disregard the position; (3) the number of times a book would be rechosen, disregarding both the individual and the position; (4) the number of times the same magazine would be placed a second time in the identical position by the same individual; (5) the number of times the same individual would rechoose a magazine but disregard the position; and (6) the number of times a magazine would be rechosen, disregarding both the individual and the position.

In answer to question 1 it was found that less than 10 per cent of the books are rechosen by the same individual in the same position; that in 23 per cent of the cases—omitting the three cases in ages 19–23—the same books are rechosen by the same individuals when we disregard the position; and finally that practically the same books are rechosen when we disregard both individuals and positions. It must be remembered that these choices were made more than six months apart and that the children in the meantime had no inkling of the fact that the questions were to be repeated. These facts point to the conclusion that since positions are not remembered one should not place too much emphasis upon the worth of the first, second, or third positions, but rather should give each position a similar or equal rating with the others.

In answering questions 4, 5, and 6, the magazines show a larger percentage of retentions of position of the same magazines, a larger percentage—38 per cent—of rechoosing of the same magazines without regard to position and a similar rechoosing of the same magazines without regard to individuals. This last fact is more cogently set forth by two lists of books and by the two lists of magazines compiled by the author but not published here.[1] In these lists it is shown that 30 magazines out of a total of 31 occurring in the first popular group were rechosen and 51 books out of 57 occurring in the first popular list were rechosen in the second. Again the summary of the lists shows that there is little variation in the type of books or magazines chosen. The facts altogether are strongly indicative (1) of a steady interest in the type of book or magazine mentioned, (2) that in some cases the book is so clearly remembered that it is given the same position in the second test as in the first one, and (3) that the type of books and the popularity of books remain approximately unchanged. The replies of children were also used, as was the case in towns 1, 2 and 3, in the study of the differences of sex, age and interest of children in reading.

Table VII was constructed to show the trends common to the four towns and cities studied. The summary table in the case of books was constructed by taking the median of the corresponding scores in the tables for the five separate censuses.[2] The median score, as in other cases, is less disturbed by the extreme measures than is the average. Thus certain classes which because of the scarcity of cases had no score whatever did not diminish the central tendency as much as would have been the case had the average been used. The scores for individual books were obtained by adding the five choices for each age in each of the four percentage tables, and then summing the four scores into one composite score. For this the tables calculated from the second test in Stuttgart were not used, since they were similar to the first. By

[1] These lists are on file in the Department of Psychology, Teachers College.
[2] The two censuses at Stuttgart were both used.

TABLE VII
CHOICES OF BOOKS. GENERAL

Choices		Age 9–11 B 59 G 87					Age 12–13 B 253 G 336					Age 14–16 B 846 G 1195					Age 17–18 B 283 G 414				
		1	2	3	4	5	1	2	3	4	5	1	2	3	4	5	1	2	3	4	5
Novels	B	4	..	2	4	4	6	7	5	5	4	20	17	17	15	14	31	31	28	24	13
	G	16	18	12	12	11	42	29	25	24	29	52	47	46	41	41	61	54	53	45	44
Stories	B	27	28	27	31	13	13	15	14	17	14	12	9	12	8	8	7	15	8	5	6
	G	72	60	68	60	63	29	41	48	42	40	28	33	28	27	33	17	7	10	11	14
Adventure	B	64	60	51	32	46	66	60	57	52	52	54	61	53	52	52	46	39	50	43	36
	G	7	6	15	11	15	18	15	12	16	18	15	18	20	21	15	15	17	17	20	10
Biography	B	2	..	7	7	..	1	2	2	3	..	1	1	..	..	1	..	..	..	2	1
	G	..	1	..	..	..	..	..	..	..	..	..	..	3	2	..	..	..	..	..	..
History	B	..	2	..	2	2	1	..	..	1	1	3	..	..	..	1	..	..	..	..	..
	G											..	1	..	1	..					
Poetry	B	..	..	..	..	..	..	2	..	..	2	..	..	..	4	2	..	..	..	2	2
	G	..	1	..	..	..	1	2	2	2	..	1	1	1	3	2	5	7	5	7	8
Science	B	..	..	..	..	..	..	..	..	1	2	..	..	..	..	..	..	..	..	..	..
	G																				
Travel	B	..	..	..	..	..	..	2	..	..	..	..	..	..	..	..	..	..	..	..	..
	G																				
Information	B	2	..	8	6	2	4	1	1	2	1	..	..	1	..	..	..	..	..	..	..
	G	..	..	..	2	1															
Humor	B	..	..	4	..	..	2	5	1	3	2	3	7	6	5	5	5	5	3	2	4
	G	1	4	..	..	..	2	2	5	..	2	2	2	3	3	1	2	..	..	..	2
Miscellaneous	B	..	..	..	..	..	..	..	..	..	..	2	3	..	2	1	4	..	..	1	2
	G	..	..	..	1	2											1	..	..	..	..
No Choice	B	..	..	..	4	14	..	..	..	..	5	..	..	3	8	11	..	1	1	8	5
	G	..	..	..	6	8	..	..	1	4	9	..	..	..	2	9	..	..	..	..	12

TREND OF ALL PLACES STUDIED

Age 19–23 B 49 G 56					9–11	SUMMARY				Grand Total	B Rank	G Rank	Per Cent of Total
1	2	3	4	5	9–11	12–13	14–16	17–18	19–23				
25	13	26	16	13	14	27	83	137	93	354	2	..	18
66	61	46	44	34	69	149	227	257	251	953	..	1	42
..	..	..	..	5	126	73	49	41	...	289	3	..	15
17	6	..	11	33	323	201	149	59	67	799	..	2	35
13	21	19	22	29	253	287	272	214	104	1130	1	..	58
11	27	32	16	16	54	79	89	79	102	403	..	3	18
..	..	..	..	..	16	8	3	3	...	30	5	..	1
..	..	..	4	..	1	...	5	...	4	10	..	6	.5
..	..	..	..	..	6	3	4	...	...	13	9	..	.6
..	..	..	..	..	...	...	2	...	...	2	..	9	..
..	5	..	..	5	...	4	6	6	...	16	7	..	.8
..	..	9	5	4	1	7	8	32	18	66	..	4	3
..	..	..	..	..	...	3	...	...	...	3	10	..	..
..	..	..	..	..	...	...	...	...	...	....	..	10	..
..	..	..	..	..	...	2	...	...	...	2	11	..	..
..	..	..	..	..	...	...	...	...	...	....	..	11	..
..	..	..	..	..	18	9	1	...	...	28	6	..	1
..	..	..	..	..	3	...	...	...	...	3	..	8	..
..	..	..	..	..	4	13	26	19	...	62	4	..	3
..	..	..	..	..	5	11	11	4	...	31	..	5	1
..	..	..	..	..	...	...	8	7	...	15	8	..	.
..	..	..	..	..	3	...	...	1	...	4	..	7	7
..	..	..	..	..	18	5	22	25	...	70	..	..	3
..	..	..	4	4	14	14	11	12	8	59	..	..	2

this method we get one score each for boys and for girls for the individual book at each age. From this list of books there were chosen eight lists, four containing the twenty most popular books for boys at each age, the other four being similar lists for girls. They are shown in Table VIII. The lists for ages 9 to 11 are poor because the number of students was so small that no extended list of popular books could be made. A much more satisfactory list for this age is given in Chapter II.

TABLE VIII

MOST POPULAR BOOKS OF THREE TOWNS AND ONE CITY ARRANGED BY SEX AND AGE

Points (Sum of First, Second, Third, Fourth, and Fifth Choices in All Municipalities) indicate relative amount of interest in each book.

Boys

Age 7-11	No. of Points	Age 12-13	No. of Points
Boy Scout Series	165	Boy Scout Series	181
Black Beauty	87	Call of the Wild	43
Robinson Crusoe	65	Treasure Island	41
Billy Whiskers	40	Motor Boy Series	24
Fairy Tales	19	Robinson Crusoe	22
Uncle Remus	14	Huckleberry Finn	22
Mrs. Wiggs of the Cabbage Patch	8	Billy Whiskers	20
History	8	Ivanhoe	18
Alice in Wonderland	7	Tom Sawyer	17
Call of the Wild	7	Penrod	16
Clansman	7	White Fang	16
Tale of Two Cities	7	Black Beauty	15
Miss Minerva and Wm. Greenhill	7	Little Men	15
Shakespeare's Works	4	Miss Minerva and Wm. Greenhill	14
Ivanhoe	4	Tale of Two Cities	13
White Fang	4	Harvester	12
History (U.S.)	4	When a Man's a Man	10
History (Ancient)	4	Kidnapped	9
Courtship of Miles Standish	4	Lady of the Lake	9
Trail of the Lonesome Pine	4	Little Women	9
Total Points	460	Total Points	526

Boys

Age 14-16	No. of Points	Age 17-18	No. of Points
Call of the Wild	106	Call of the Wild	147
Treasure Island	71	Tale of Two Cities	59
Boy Scout Series	42	Tom Sawyer	55
Tom Sawyer	41	Ivanhoe	38
Ivanhoe	39	Huckleberry Finn	37
Kidnapped	32	When a Man's a Man	37
Huckleberry Finn	31	Boy Scout Series	30
Tale of Two Cities	23	Treasure Island	29
When a Man's a Man	22	Trail of the Lonesome Pine	27
White Fang	21	David Copperfield	26
Freckles	20	Lorna Doone	24
Penrod	20	Freckles	23
Little Shepherd of Kingdom Come	17	Little Shepherd of Kingdom Come	23
Sherlock Holmes	17	Shepherd of the Hills	21
Swiss Family Robinson	15	Lady of the Lake	20
Motor Boy Series	12	White Fang	20
Lady of the Lake	12	Virginian	18
Shepherd of the Hills	12	Graustark	18
Robinson Crusoe	12	Robinson Crusoe	17
Lorna Doone	11	Penrod	17
Total Points	576	Total Points	686

Girls

Age 9-11	No. of Points	Age 12-13	No. of Points
Black Beauty	88	Pollyanna	64
Little Women	54	Freckles	55
Little Colonel Series	48	Little Women	53
Little Men	48	Fairy Tales	51
Old Fashioned Girl	34	Girl of the Limberlost	51
Daddy Takes Us to the Circus	32	Anne of Green Gables	35
Fairy Tales	30	Elsie Dinsmore	33
Girl of the Limberlost	29	Rebecca of Sunnybrook Farm	31
Anne of Green Gables	19	Boy Scouts	30
Billy Whiskers	18	Laddie	28
Camp Fire Girls	18	Little Colonel Series	27
Harvester	17	Little Pepper Series	24
Alice in Wonderland	17	Ben Hur	22
Robinson Crusoe	14	Black Beauty	15

	No. of Points		No. of Points
Helen's Babies	13	Miss Minerva and Wm. Greenhill	13
Little Pepper Series	12	Life of Lincoln	13
Bunny Brown and His Sister Sue	12	Tom Sawyer	12
Shakespeare	8	Just David	12
Boy Scouts Series	8	Little Men	11
Rebecca of Sunnybrook Farm	8	Last of the Mochicans	11
Total Points	**527**	**Total Points**	**591**

Girls

Age 14-16	No. of Points	Age 17-18	No. of Points
Little Women	69	Tale of Two Cities	62
Pollyanna	57	Girl of the Limberlost	58
Girl of the Limberlost	56	David Copperfield	43
Freckles	56	Shepherd of the Hills	43
Ivanhoe	33	Freckles	39
Eyes of the World	29	Ivanhoe	38
Tale of Two Cities	27	When a Man's a Man	38
Laddie	26	Trail of the Lonesome Pine	32
Rebecca of Sunnybrook Farm	25	Little Women	31
David Copperfield	24	Call of the Wild	30
Camp Fire Girls	24	Eyes of the World	26
Shepherd of the Hills	23	Lady of the Lake	24
Little Shepherd of Kingdom Come	22	Little Shepherd of Kingdom Come	23
Little Colonel Series	21	Ben Hur	22
Trail of the Lonesome Pine	20	Laddie	20
Harvester	19	Merchant of Venice	20
Seventeen	17	Silas Marner	19
Secret Garden	16	Anne of Green Gables	17
Tom Sawyer	16	Mill on the Floss	17
Lorna Doone	15	Lorna Doone	16
Total Points	**594**	**Total Points**	**618**

Both boys and girls show a very large interest in fiction in comparison with that shown in other types. Girls like fiction best of all. Boys place it second only to adventure. The seven most popular books for boys are: *When a Man's a Man, Freckles, Little Shepherd of Kingdom Come, Penrod, Lorna Doone, Shepherd of the Hills,* and *Trail of the Lonesome*

Pine. The following are the seven most popular books for girls: *Girl of the Limberlost, Freckles, Polyanna, Laddie, Anne of Green Gables, David Copperfield,* and *Shepherd of the Hills.*

There is, moreover, an increasing interest in fiction among both boys and girls from 9–19 years. The greatest change in this interest among boys takes place between the years 12–13 and 14–16. In addition, there is an increase approximately equal to the foregoing from 14–16 to 17–18. In the case of girls the increase of interest is greatest between the years 9–11 and 12–13.

Boys choose books classed as juvenile fiction only less often than adventure and fiction. The large number of these choices, however, is made during the years 9-13. For these years juvenile fiction ranks ahead of adult fiction and second only to adventure. This type of fiction constitutes 15 per cent of the total for boys and 35 per cent of the total for girls. Girls choose juvenile fiction second only to adult fiction and during the years 9–11 choose the former most of all. The seven most popular books for boys are: *Black Beauty, Billy Whiskers,* Fairy Tales, *Little Men, Uncle Remus, Little Women,* and *Mrs. Wiggs of the Cabbage Patch.* The seven books most often chosen by girls are: *Little Women, Black Beauty,* Little Colonel Series, Fairy Tales, *Little Men,* Little Pepper Series, and *The Old Fashioned Girl.*

Boys and girls show a marked decrease in the amount of interest in juvenile fiction from 9–11 to 12–13. This interest decreases throughout the high-school period until at 17–18 years juvenile fiction forms only a minor part of the choices of the children. Noteworthy is the fact that the drop in interest in juvenile fiction is accompanied by the rise of interest in adult fiction. In the case of both boys and girls juvenile fiction is chosen more times than is adult fiction between the years 9–13, but thereafter adult fiction leads with both sexes.

Adventure is chosen by the boys more than three times as often as fiction, and more times at every age than any other type. In fact, this class of reading receives 58 per cent of the total votes of the boys. Girls by their choices show that their interest in adventure is next in amount to that in juvenile fiction. For boys the most popular books are: Boy Scout Series, *Call of the Wild, Treasure Island, Robinson Crusoe, Tale of Two Cities, Ivanhoe,* and *White Fang.* The seven most popular books for girls are: *Tale of Two Cities, Camp Fire Girls, Ivanhoe, Boy Scouts, Alice in Wonderland, Robinson Crusoe,* and *The Last of the Mohicans.* In every age boys are far more interested in adventure than girls are. There is an increase of interest in adventure among boys from the years 9–11 to 12–13, and after that a gradual decrease up to 18 years of age. The interest of girls in this type increases up to the years 14–16 and then decreases.

Since the interest in biography and history is so small, they may well be treated together. Boys choose a very small number of books of biography—slightly over one per cent; girls practically none except at the age of 14–16. This does not mean that boys and girls have no interest whatsoever in biography but only that books of biography are not chosen by them with sufficient frequency to warrant their being placed on the most popular lists, except in one case where 12–13-year-old girls choose *The Life of Lincoln.* Boys choose biography three times as frequently as do girls. There is a decrease of interest in biography among boys as the years advance. There is a very small interest in history among the boys—.6 of one per cent—and practically none at all among the girls.

There is a small interest in poetry in the case of both boys and girls. It constitutes .8 of one per cent of the total number of books chosen by boys and 3 per cent of the total number of books chosen by girls thus indicating the greater popularity of poetry among girls. Shakespeare's Works, *The Merchant of Venice*, and *The Lady of the Lake* constitute the poetry most frequently chosen by boys and girls. Girls show a small increase in their number of votes for poetry up to their 16th year, and then at 17-18 a substantial increase.

Books on travel and science need not concern us here, since the interest is less than one per cent.

There is a small interest in books on information at 9-11 and 12-13 years among the boys—somewhat more than one per cent.

There is a substantial interest in humor in the case of boys after the eleventh year. Girls from 12-16 show a small interest in humor also. The small percentages of the other types of books in Table VII indicate a comparative lack of interest. For example, books on travel and science show the smallest per cent of all, making apparent an appalling lack of interest in these desirable subjects. Books on information fare only a little better, although among boys from 9-13 years some interest does appear. Humor is also attractive to both boys and girls, but more so to boys than to girls. The attention shown to this type of book warrants listing here those most often mentioned. They are: *Tom Sawyer*, *Huckleberry Finn*, and *Miss Minerva and William Greenhill*. Girls like only *Tom Sawyer* and *Miss Minerva and William Greenhill*.

The classifications of magazines in some instances are less clearly cut than are those of the books. This fact is apparent when we attempt to separate fiction and "woman's arts" on the one hand and adventure and "science" on the other. One could almost as well have classed fiction as a larger group with "woman's arts" as a subhead under it and adventure as a larger group and "science" as a subhead under that. This fact of overlapping classifications must be kept in mind in considering the choice of fiction, which often forms a large part of the magazines in woman's arts as well as of fiction proper.

Both boys and girls evince a deep interest in magazines of fiction. This interest in the case of boys ranks second only to adventure and in the case of girls second only to woman's arts. The following magazines of the fiction group are those most popular with boys: *Saturday Evening Post*, *Cosmopolitan*, *American Magazine*, and the *Red Book*. The four magazines of this type most popular with girls are: *Cosmopolitan*, *American Magazine*, *Saturday Evening Post* and *Harper's*. The percentages chosen at each age are as follows:

Age	9-11	12-13	14-16	17-18
Boys	7	9	17	27
Girls	8	14	25	37

It appears from the above percentages that girls are more interested in magazines of fiction than boys are. It may also be noted that this interest increases steadily from age 9 to 18.

Boys and girls choose a small number of magazines classed as juvenile fiction during the years 9 to 16. The number chosen by boys constitutes 6 per cent of the total during these ages, while girls choose 4 per cent. The only two magazines to any extent popular with boys are *Boy's Life* and *Little Folks*. Those popular among girls are *St. Nicholas*, *Little Folks Magazine*, and *Boys and Girls Magazine*. The number chosen decreases rather rapidly, and at eighteen years scores have disappeared from the table of the girls and almost from that of the boys.

Magazines of adventure, just as books of adventure, lead all other magazines in the number of times chosen in case of the boys. Indeed the interest in adventure is so great that those classed as adventure are about 29 per cent of the total. Here we find the most significant differences between boys and girls, for the latter choose only 6 per cent.

Percentages at the several ages show the declining interest of both boys and girls after 12-13 years.

Age	9-11	12-13	14-16	17-18
Boys	36	29	26	15
Girls	9	10	5	4

The *American Boy* heads the list of magazines of adventure. With boys it is the most popular of all types of magazines. Next to it, but a poor second, is *The Youth's Companion*, and far behind it the *Boy Scout Magazine*. The *Youth's Companion*, however, is of approximately equal interest to both boys and girls.

The *Country Gentleman* and the *National Geographic* appeal more strongly to boys than to girls. The former choose about 4 per cent of the whole of their magazine reading from among such journals while the girls choose only .7 of 1 per cent. Boys' interests increase from 9-18 in this class, but that of girls begins at 12-13, rises a little, and then declines.

Magazines made up largely of pictures, such as the *Pictorial Review*, *Photoplay*, and *Motion Pictures*, and those concerned with woman's arts appeal almost exclusively to girls. The first group includes 7 per cent of the total, the second group 40 per cent. Among this latter group *The Ladies Home Journal, Woman's Home Companion, Woman's World*, and the *Delineator* lead the list. Woman's arts then receive the lion's share of interest. Percentages at various ages for both boys and girls are interesting:

Age	9-11	12-13	14-16	17-18
Boys	12	4	2	4
Girls	39	37	37	30

Results of the Questionnaire

It will be noticed that girls are tremendously interested in woman's arts and that this interest falls off just a little. Of course, the fact that the magazine is taken in the home works a tremendous influence, and the boys and girls questioned might think of those they had seen last. I do not believe children at 9–11 are so interested in woman's arts as these percentages indicate. On the other hand, girls observed in public libraries did not as a rule frequent the magazine tables, and therefore must have had no vital interest in them. The fact remains that there is something about the make-up of the *Ladies Home Journal*, the *Woman's Home Companion*, and similar magazines which appeals strongly to girls. Boys also show some interest in this group, although the interest is small.

Magazines of a scientific nature claim a considerable following among boys, being about 16 per cent of the whole, while that of girls is 2 per cent. *Popular Mechanics* is far and away ahead of all other magazines. *Popular Science* and the *Scientific American* come in for a good share of interest, but both of these combined hardly poll more than one fourth of the votes cast for *Popular Mechanics*. The following table of percentages shows something of this interest when considered as a whole:

Age	9-11	12-13	14-16	17-18
Boys	4	19	19	25
Girls	3	14	1	2

One cannot afford to overlook the tremendous growth of interest from 9–11 to 12–13 and from 14–16 to 17–18 among boys. When we consider that these are total choices we can readily understand the importance of this large interest.

Not less significant to the student of education is the interest of both boys and girls in magazines dealing with current events for these constitute 9 per cent of the total number of choices with boys and 7 per cent in the case of girls. The magazines in this group most popular with boys are the *Literary Digest, Collier's,* the *Review of Reviews,* and the *Independent;* the girls enjoy practically the same ones. The percentages below show the differences between boys and girls, and the changes in their interests.

Age	*9-11*	*12-13*	*14-16*	*17-18*
Boys	1	6	12	13
Girls	2	2	7	17

There are a few magazines of humor, such as *Life,* which seem to be interesting to a very small percentage of boys and girls between the ages of 13-18.

TABLE IX
MOST POPULAR MAGAZINES, FAYETTEVILLE, ARK., LAWRENCE, KAN., STUTTGART, ARK., WASHINGTON, D.C.
Points = Sum of Choices, 1,2,3, in all four cities

Boys

Age 9-11	No. of Points	*Age 12-13*	No. of Points
American Boy	107	American Boy	199
Popular Science	90	Popular Mechanics	180
Youth's Companion	57	Youth's Companion	115
Country Gentleman	44	Popular Science	54
Boy Scouts	43	Literary Digest	52
Woman's Home Companion	33	Boys Life	47
Literary Digest	25	Ladies' Home Journal	29
Boys' Magazine	21	Saturday Evening Post	28
Little Folks	15	National Geographic	26
McCall's	14	Reviews of Reviews	22
Saturday Evening Post	11	Life	20
Cosmopolitan	11	St. Nicholas	20
Something To Do	8	Cosmopolitan	20
American Magazine	7	Boy Scout	18
Total Points	486	Total Points	830

Results of the Questionnaire

Boys

Age 14-16	No. of Points	Age 17-18	No. of Points
American Boy	179	Popular Mechanics	161
Popular Mechanics	122	Literary Digest	96
Literary Digest	82	American Boy	91
Youth's Companion	71	Saturday Evening Post	71
Saturday Evening Post	50	American Magazine	50
American Magazine	36	Cosmopolitan	46
Popular Science	35	Youth's Companion	46
Cosmopolitan	30	Collier's	28
Boys Life	26	Life	26
Life	25	Scientific American	26
National Geographic	23	Country Gentleman	25
Red Book	23	National Geographic	22
Collier's	16	Popular Science	22
Everybody's	15	Independent	22
Total Points	733	Total Points	732

Girls

Age 9-11	No. of Points	Age 12-13	No. of Points
Ladies' Home Journal	175	Ladies' Home Journal	199
Youth's Companion	77	St. Nicholas	110
Pictorial Review	62	Youth's Companion	105
St. Nicholas	46	Pictorial Review	71
Little Folks	35	Woman's Home Companion	42
Woman's World	32	Cosmopolitan	36
Woman's Home Companion	29	Saturday Evening Post	30
Literary Digest	28	Literary Digest	28
McCalls	27	Delineator	26
American Magazine	20	Woman's World	26
Harper's	17	American Boy	22
Popular Mechanics	17	Life	20
Something To Do	12	Little Folks	20
Boys and Girls	6	Red Book	18
Total Points	576	Total Points	753

Girls

Age 14-16	No. of Points	Age 17-18	No. of Points
Ladies' Home Journal	178	Ladies' Home Journal	169
Cosmopolitan	72	Literary Digest	102
American Magazine	61	Cosmopolitan	78
Youth's Companion	58	American Magazine	59
Pictorial Review	55	Good Housekeeping	59
Woman's Home Companion	53	Saturday Evening Post	56
Literary Digest	51	Harper's	45
Saturday Evening Post	46	Woman's Home Companion	45
Woman's World	39	Youth's Companion	40
Delineator	39	National Geographic	31
St. Nicholas	35	Pictorial Review	31
Harper's	31	Delineator	30
Red Book	30	Woman's World	29
McCall's	23	Life	28
Total Points	771	Total Points	802

Validity of Results Obtained By Questioning Children

There are several possible sources of error in data collected by means of questioning pupils. (*a*) Children are likely to write down what is expected of them and not what they really like, and may write nothing when some real preference exists which they prefer not to reveal. (*b*) The choices are too greatly influenced by what the children read in school.

We admit that the effect of the school situation in our inquiry was to dignify the types of books and magazines chosen, but, in our opinion, the discount made necessary by this fact is not large. In the first place, unusual pains were taken to prevent this factor from influencing the results. Children were told clearly that their replies would not be used against them. In two cases, Fayetteville, Arkansas, and Lawrence, Kansas, the data were collected by a stranger to the pupils who assured them that their replies would not be shown to their teachers. Again, the pupils were asked to write only their first names. As a result of these precautions the attitude of the pupils was excellent. They performed the work willingly, earnestly, and at times eagerly. Only in rare instances did they make play of the questions.

In the second place factor (*a*) was not strong enough to cause many choices of Shakespeare or Shelley, Keats or Byron or Wordsworth. One does not find among the lists of popular books in Fayetteville *The House of Seven Gables*, although it was studied in that school. Moreover, many of the books appearing in the children's replies were most certainly not desirable and not literature in any sense of the word. There were cases of *Jesse James*, *Three Weeks*, *Dick Merriwell*, and *Nick Carter* among the boys and enough votes from girls for *Elsie Dinsmore*, the goody-goody variety of book, to place it on the popular lists. The very large popularity of *Pollyanna*, H. B. Wright's works, and Gene Stratton Porter's is evidence of truth-telling by the pupils. There is a final point which needs emphasis—the attitude of the pupils.

The total percentage of boys who had no choice of books was 3 per cent of the whole, and less than 5 per cent in the case of magazines. The total percentage of girls who had no choice of books was less than 2 per cent of the whole, and 5 per cent in the case of magazines. Before we can use the percentages as indicators of a poorer type of reading, there must be subtracted from these comparatively small numbers the percentages of those who were very fond of many books and for this reason could not make a choice.

In Lawrence, Kansas, there were 56 books out of 72 on the list most frequently chosen which were not used either in school or recommended by it for collateral reading, and at Washington, D. C., there were 41 books out of 87 on the popular lists which were not used in school or recommended by it for collateral reading. Among the magazines only the *Literary Digest*, the *Independent*, and the *Review of Reviews* were consistently used and recommended by the schools studied. The fact that a book is used in school insures its being read by comparatively large numbers; and even if only a small proportion of users like it, its position of popularity will be relatively too high. On the whole, the influence of the school situation, of the school reading, and of the omission of choices of books and magazines probably was to make the choices of books and magazines somewhat, but not much, more dignified than they would otherwise have been.

SUMMARY

The major interests of boys will first be treated. Boys choose both books and magazines of adventure most frequently of all. So great is this interest that in the case of books this type comprises 58 per cent of the total choices and a majority of choices at every age. The extraordinary appeal of *The Call of the Wild*, the Boy Scout Series, and *Treasure Island* is a further indication of the greatness of this interest. Of the magazines of adventure, the *American Boy* is the most popular with boys. Akin to this interest in adventure is that in the popular presentation of scientific subjects. Boys show a large interest in magazines of this sort but practically none in books of science. *Popular Mechanics*, one of the magazines of this group, ranks second in interest only to the *American Boy*. Second only to this enormous interest in adventure is that in fiction. This is ranked second among boys in both magazines and books. Books of fiction receive 18 per cent of the boys' total vote, which may be compared with the 58 per cent for adventure. Magazines of fiction, on the other hand, get 24 per cent of the boys' total vote while magazines of adventure obtain 29 per cent. In addition, boys have considerable interest in juvenile fiction which ranks third with books and sixth with magazines. Humor receives 3 per cent of the total choices. Their interest in books of biography, history, poetry, and information is small, less than 4 per cent of the total number of choices. The number of points in travel and science is less than 1 per cent. Finally, magazines concerned with current events receive 9 per cent of the total choices of boys for magazines; woman's arts, 6 per cent; nature, 4 per cent; humor, 4 per cent; and pictures, 2 per cent.

Girls choose books and magazines of fiction far more frequently than they do those of any other type. The number of choices given fiction ranks first in books and second in magazines. Among magazines the woman's arts magazines are most attractive since they contain both popular fiction as well as a treatment of woman's arts. If this is understood, fiction stands out preeminently in the interest of girls. (Further evidence of the amount of interest in fiction is the occurrence of 18 books of fiction in the four lists of the five most popular books with girls for each town. Again, *Little Women* leads the lists of popular books for girls in two cities. *Pollyanna* leads the corresponding list of another, while *The Girl of the Limberlost* leads the fourth. *The Girl of the Limberlost* occurs in all four lists of the five most popular books for girls.) Among books this classification receives 41 per cent of the total, while in magazines it receives 27 per cent, and in addition woman's arts, which is partly fiction, receive 40 per cent of the total number of choices. Juvenile fiction in books, which obtained 35 per cent of the total choices, ranks second in interest. Among magazines this type ranks sixth. If we add together the points for adult fiction and juvenile fiction in the case of books the result comprises 77 per cent of the total number, and if we add the points for fiction, juvenile fiction, and woman's arts in magazines, the result is 70 per cent of the total. Again, girls have a substantial interest in books of adventure, 18 per cent, and a smaller interest in magazines of this type, 6 per cent. The choices for poetry constitute 3 per cent of the total number of choices. Biography, history, travel, information, humor and miscellaneous amount to approximately 2 per cent of the whole number. Of the remaining types of magazines current events receives 12 per cent of the choices; pictures, 7 per cent; science, 2 per cent; humor, .8 of 1 per cent; and nature, .7 of 1 per cent.

Boys and girls show essentially different emphases in their interests in reading in the case of both books and magazines. Boys are far more interested than girls in both books and magazines which deal with adventure. On the other hand, girls are more attracted by fiction, both adult and juvenile, in books and by adult fiction in magazines. Boys choose most often *The Call of the Wild*, Boy Scout Series, and *Treasure Island*,—all books of adventure; girls choose most frequently *Little Women, Girl of the Limberlost*, and *Pollyanna*,—all books of fiction. In some instances, such as in the case of *Ivanhoe* and *The Tale of Two Cities*, the facts seem to warrant the conclusion that even in these cases the boys enjoy these books for war, rivalry, and action; the girls for the sentiment, kindliness, and emotion. The differences are also clearly shown in the choices of magazines among which boys choose far more than girls those of adventure and scientific subjects; while girls choose more often than boys magazines of woman's arts, and of pictures, which deal at least in part with woman's arts. Boys and girls are alike in their failure to choose to any large extent books on science, information, travel, biography, and history, and magazines on humor and nature. Their interests in current events up to the age of 18 are also somewhat similar. During the years 12–13 the differences between the sexes is greatest. At this age girls choose books of fiction more than five times as often as do boys and juvenile books almost three times as often. Boys, for their part, choose adventure almost four times as frequently as do girls. In addition, they choose magazines of science 22 times as often. Girls at this age choose pictorial magazines 13 times as often as do boys. There are a number of changes in the interests of both boys and girls. The interest in fiction increases rapidly in the case of both boys and girls in both magazines and books from 9–18 years. The greatest increase in the percentage of fiction with boys comes between the ages 14–16 and 17–18; the greatest increase with girls between the ages 9–11 and 12–13. In magazines, the greatest increase in interest comes with boys between the years 14–16 and 17–18; with girls, the greatest increase comes at the same age. Books of juvenile fiction rapidly decline in interest for both boys and girls. The greatest decline in both sexes takes place between the years 9–11 and 12–13. In magazines, the number of choices of juvenile fiction decreases in the case of both boys and girls from 9 to 18 years. Girls show the greatest decrease from 14–16 to 17–18; boys, between the years 12–13 and 14–16. The remaining most significant changes in interest in books are, in the case of boys, first, in adventure, in increase in the percentages between the years 9–11 and 12–13, followed by a decrease; and, second, a rapid increase of interest in science between the years 9–11 and 12–13, then a slight decline followed by another increase; and, finally, the rapid and continued rise of interest in current events from 9 to 18 years. Girls, aside from fiction, show some important changes of interest. Some of the most important of these are, in the case of books, first, a substantial increase from 9–11 to 12–13 in the percentages of adventure chosen; and, second, a corresponding rise in interest in poetry from 14–16 to 17–18. In the case of magazines girls show, first, a rapid decrease of interest in pictures from the years 9–11 to 12–13 and also from 14–16 to 17–18; second, a small decline of interest in woman's arts from 9 to 18; and, finally, a most rapid increase of interest in current events from the years 14–16 to 17–18.

CHAPTER IV

LATER INVESTIGATIONS BY THE METHOD OF THE QUESTIONNAIRE

During the years 1917-1918 the writer made an investigation of children's interests in reading. It consisted first of an enquiry consisting of questions to be answered which related to the five books and three magazines that pupils of high school age and below liked best. Moreover, the children's rooms of several public libraries in and around New York City were visited and records kept of the books and magazines which the children were reading and which they chose when left to their own volition. Letters were sent to publishers in the hope of finding some circulation figures which might throw light on what books and magazines boys and girls actually like. Thus the old.

The new material was collected in the year 1925 from the cities of Charlotte and Greensboro[1] both in the state of North Carolina. The principals of the high schools had given to all those present on one day the same questionnaire that was previously given to pupils in Fayetteville and Stuttgart, Arkansas; Lawrence, Kansas; and Washington, D. C. The questionnaire follows.

I. 1. Will you kindly write down for me the name of the book you like best of all the books you have ever read?

[1] These two cities of about the same size (50,000) are located in the Piedmont section of North Carolina. Life in each city has been quickened by the development in recent years of various types of industries both within and without their city limits. Concomitantly with these enterprises there has developed an increased interest in schools and in other types of education. Both municipalities today are no longer merely small towns but quite modern cities.

2. Will you write down for me the name of the book you like next best of all the books you have ever read?
3. Will you write down the name of the book you like next best, and next best of all the books you have ever read until you have written five books arranged in order of your preference?

II. 1. Will you write down for me the name of the magazine you like best of all the magazines you have ever read?
2. Will you write down the name of the magazine you like next best of all the magazines you have ever read?
3. Will you write down for me the name of the magazine you like next best of all the magazines you have ever read so that altogether you have written three magazines arranged in the order of your preference?

In this manner reports were obtained from 1559 high school pupils, 695 of whom were boys and 864 were girls. We have here sufficient data for comparison with the results obtained seven or eight years earlier. Such questions as the following may now be asked: Do children's interests change very greatly from time to time and from place to place? What effect does a good library have upon their choices of books and magazines? How well do children like these modern books? What effect does living in a different part of the country have on their choice of books?

Let us now consider the case of the magazines. Table X, which includes the data from both Greensboro and Charlotte, sets forth the percentage of each general type of magazine chosen by boys and girls.

The number choosing certain types is immediately apparent. With boys, adventure and fiction lead; but there are evidences of considerable interest in magazines dealing in a popular way with scientific subjects. Five to ten per cent say that they like magazines concerned with current events, while about 5 per cent choose those concerned with nature.

TABLE X
TYPES OF MAGAZINES ARRANGED BY AGE AND SEX. PERCENTAGE TABLE DATA INCLUDE BOTH CHARLOTTE AND GREENSBORO.

Age		12-13	14-16	17-18
Number	B	62	484	149
	G	99	568	197
Adult Fiction	B	18.5	27.4	41.8
	G	30.7	41.1	40.2
Juvenile Fiction	B	17.9	9.3	3.8
	G	10.7	1.1	
Adventure	B	21.2	11.4	7.8
	G	2.3	1.8	1.0
Nature	B	5.2	5.3	5.1
	G	2.5	3.3	2.7
Pictures	B	.4	1.7	2.1
	G	10.3	10.3	5.5
Woman's Arts	B	3.4	1.4	1.1
	G	24.2	21.8	25.4
Science	B	17.8	16.7	13.3
	G	3.0	1.3	.6
Current Events	B	5.6	8.3	11.5
	G	5.1	8.6	15.7
Humor	B	2.6	8.0	8.2
	G	5.8	5.3	3.9
Miscellaneous	B	2.3	4.6	4.8
	G	3.8	3.2	3.1
No Choice	B	4.4	6.3	0.0
	G	1.4	2.8	1.9
Per Cent	B	100.0	100.0	100.0
	G	100.0	100.0	100.0

Magazines dealing largely with simple stories appeal quite strongly during the earlier years of high school but this appeal decreases as the pupils grow older. Note that about 5 per cent of the boys during the first three years in high school do not like magazines well enough to fill out the three choices.

Changes in boys' interests in some cases are quite noticeable. For example, the number choosing fiction begins with

18 per cent for the years 12–13, but jumps to 42 per cent for the years 17–18; that is, more than doubled. On the other hand the percentage choosing stories drops from 18 per cent to three during the same period. Interest in magazines of adventure and science decreases noticeably during the high school period, while there is a decided increase in magazines dealing with current events and humor. Magazines dealing with nature remain about the same.

Girls choose most frequently magazines dealing with fiction and with woman's arts. These two constitute a good deal more than half of the total number of magazines listed. If we add to these the periodicals dealing with pictures, for these too are mostly of woman's arts, we have nearly three fourths of the total number of magazines. The number of girls choosing magazines of nature, adventure, and science is almost negligible. In current events and humor there is shown small amount of interest. Story magazines appeal during the years 12–13 but not later. About 2 per cent of the girls do not like magazines sufficiently well to fill out all three choices to which they were entitled.

There are some substantial changes of interest during the high school period. Even though 30 per cent of the girls at ages 12–13 say they like magazines of fiction, this number increases to 41 per cent at 14–16 years and remains about the same during the years 17–18. The type known as woman's arts, changes only slightly during the high school period. Magazines dealing with current events change from 5 per cent at 12–13 to 15 per cent at the ages 17–18. Pictures, adventure, and humor increase only slightly. The percentage choosing magazines of nature remains approximately the same from years 12–18.

Boys and girls differ rather widely in their interests. These differences are most clearly seen in woman's arts, in science, and in adventure. While more than 20 per cent of girls choose magazines of woman's arts, less than 2 per cent of boys choose this type. Boys select about 15 per cent of magazines of science; girls less than 2 per cent. In the upper years this interest in the case of girls has almost entirely disappeared. Similar conditions are found with magazines of adventure which more than 10 per cent of the boys choose and which less than 2 per cent of girls choose. Magazines composed largely of pictures are chosen mostly by girls since picture magazines portray women and woman's arts to a very large extent. The largest difference between boys and girls in magazines of fiction occurs at the years 12-13 and 14-16, but at the years 17-18 this difference in interest has almost disappeared. Except with the years 17-18 three times as many boys as girls do not like magazines well enough to choose three of them.

One of the most astonishing things in the first investigation was the unusual similarity of choices among books in places so dissimilar as Fayetteville, Arkansas, and Washington, D. C., or Newark, New Jersey. (Data from Newark collected but not published.) It therefore seemed interesting to compare those of 1917 with these of 1925 in cities as different as Lawrence, Kansas and Greensboro, North Carolina. It would have been better to have had the same questions given in the same high school on successive occasions in which case the differences in preferences would probably have been smaller than in the present instant.

Table XI on the opposite page sets forth the likenesses and differences in preferences for magazines in case of boys.

There are some rather striking quantitative differences. In the 1917 groups there were almost twice as many magazines of adventure chosen, and more of them treating of science in a popular way. On the other hand, the boys of Greensboro and Charlotte in 1925 choose magazines of fiction much more frequently than those of 1917. On the average 18.7

Table XI
COMPARISON OF THE PREFERENCES OF BOYS FOR MAGAZINES FROM DATA COLLECTED EIGHT YEARS APART IN WIDELY SEPARATED CITIES

B1 = Boys of Greensboro and Charlotte 1925.
B2 = Boys of Washington, Stuttgart and Fayetteville Ark., and Lawrence Kan. 1917.

Age		*12-13*	*14-16*	*17-18*
Number	B1	62	484	149
	B2	353	846	283
Adult Fiction	B1	18.5	27.4	41.8
	B2	9.8	18.1	28.3
Juvenile Fiction	B1	17.9	9.3	3.8
	B2	7.0	4.1	3.1
Adventure	B1	21.2	11.4	7.8
	B2	30.8	26.9	15.5
Nature	B1	5.2	5.3	5.1
	B2	4.2	4.4	5.2
Pictures	B1	.4	1.7	2.1
	B2	.7	2.4	0.0
Woman's Arts	B1	3.4	1.4	1.1
	B2	4.5	2.0	4.5
Science	B1	17.8	16.7	13.3
	B2	20.3	19.1	25.5
Current Events	B1	5.6	8.3	11.5
	B2	6.3	11.9	13.8
Humor	B1	2.6	8.0	8.2
	B2	3.5	2.7	3.1
Miscellaneous	B1	2.3	4.6	4.8
	B2	3.1	1.4	1.3
No Choice	B1	4.4	6.3	0.0
	B2	9.4	6.8	0.0
Per Cent	B1	100.0	100.0	100.0
	B2	100.0	100.0	100.0

choose fiction in 1917 while 29.2 chose it in 1925. It seems that these latter are reading less, *Popular Mechanics*, *Popular Science*, and the *American Boy* and more the *American*, *Saturday Evening Post*, and *True Story*. Among the other types the similarities are more noticeable than the differences, although the boys of Greensboro and Charlotte do read more humor than those of Lawrence, Kansas, or Washington, D. C. The five most popular magazines in each investigation bring out the same differences.

TABLE XII

FIVE MAGAZINES MOST POPULAR WITH BOYS

Age	12-13	14-16	17-18
First Investigation 1917	American Boy Popular Mechanics Youth's Companion Popular Science Literary Digest	American Boy Popular Mechanics Literary Digest Youth's Companion Sat. Evening Post	Popular Mechanics Literary Digest American Boy Sat. Evening Post American Magazine
Second Investigation 1925	American Boy Boys Life American Magazine Popular Science Popular Mechanics	American Magazine American Boy Boy's Life Popular Mechanics Literary Digest	America Magazine Literary Digest Sat. Evening Post American Boy Cosmopolitan

Thus it seems that the *American Magazine* in the cities of Greensboro and Charlotte is the leading magazine with the boys at the years 14–18. On the other hand the *American Boy* up to the years 14–16 is undoubtedly full of interest. Even in Greensboro and Charlotte in 1925 the difference in the number of choices between the *American Magazine* and the *American Boy* is only slightly in favor of the former.

The most striking thing about Table XIII is the similarity between the figures for the two groups. (See opposite page.) Only in three cases are the differences significant. The 1925 groups of girls do not like adventure nearly so well as the 1917 groups. Moreover, the 1925 groups read considerably more fiction during the years 12–16 and less of Womans Arts. And finally, the girls of Charlotte and Greensboro, like the boys, read more magazines of humor than those of 1917. The five most popular magazines at each age, Table XIV, set forth a similar situation.

TABLE XIII
COMPARISON OF THE PREFERENCES OF GIRLS FOR MAGAZINES FROM DATA COLLECTED EIGHT YEARS APART IN WIDELY SEPARATED CITIES.
G1 = Girls of Greensboro and Charlotte 1925
G2 = Girls of Washington, Stuttgart and Fayetteville, Arkansas and Lawrence, Kansas, 1917.

Age		12-13	14-16	17-18
Number	G1	99	568	197
	G2	336	1195	414
Adult Fiction	G1	30.7	41.1	40.9
	G2	15.3	27.0	38.8
Juvenile Fiction	G1	10.7	1.0	0.0
	G2	8.2	3.9	0.0
Adventure	G1	2.3	1.8	.9
	G2	11.6	5.4	4.2
Nature	G1	2.5	3.3	2.7
	G2	1.1	1.4	1.1
Pictures	G1	10.3	10.3	5.5
	G2	10.1	8.3	.4
Woman's Arts	G1	24.2	21.8	25.4
	G2	41.4	39.6	32.5
Science	G1	3.0	1.3	.65
	G2			
Current Events	G1	5.1	8.6	15.7
	G2	2.6	7.2	17.6
Humor	G1	5.7	5.2	3.9
	G2	1.9	1.4	.7
Miscellaneous	G1	3.8	3.2	3.1
	G2	.8	1.1	.7
No Choice	G1	1.4	2.8	2.0
	G2	6.3	3.2	2.1
Per Cent	G1	100.0	100.0	100.0
	G2	100.0	100.0	100.0

TABLE XIV
FIVE MAGAZINES MOST POPULAR WITH GIRLS

Age	12-13	14-16	17-18
First Investigation	Ladies Home Journal	Ladies Home Journal	Ladies Home Journal
	Saint Nicholas	Cosmopolitan	Literary Digest
	Youths Companion	American Magazine	Cosmopolitan
	Pictorial Review	Youths Companion	American Magazine
	Womans Home Companion	Pictorial Review	Good Housekeeping

Second Investigation	American Magazine Ladies Home Journal Good Housekeeping Pictorial Review McCalls	American Magazine Ladies Home Journal Cosmopolitan Good Housekeeping Literary Digest	American Magazine Literary Digest Ladies Home Journal Cosmopolitan Good Housekeeping

The *American Magazine* seems to have displaced the *Ladies Home Journal* as the most popular magazine for girls during the high school age. Otherwise there are more similarities than differences.

Perhaps a more complete picture of the differences between the results of the former investigation and those of the present one may be had by listing first the most popular magazines of the two cities in the recent investigation, and then, by referring to page 44 we may compare these results with those of the first investigation.

TABLE XV
MOST POPULAR MAGAZINES OF CHARLOTTE AND GREENSBORO
Boys Points=Sum of first, second, and third choices

Age	*12–13*		*14–16*		*17–18*	
Number	62		484		149	
	American Boy		28 American Magazine	182	American Magazine	96
	Boys Life		22 American Boy	172	Literary Digest	42
	American		18 Boys Life	122	Saturday Evening Post	34
	Popular Science		16 Popular Mechanics	93	American Boy	30
	Popular Mechanics		13 Literary Digest	88	Cosmopolitan	23
	National Geographic		11 Popular Science	82	Popular Mechanics	21
	Literary Digest		11 Sat. Evening Post	72	National Geographic	15
	Sat. Evening Post		10 National Geographic	56	Life	15
	Ladies Home Journal		6 Life	37	Boys Life	14
	Youths Companion		4 Cosmopolitan	30	Collier's	7
	Life		4 Red Book	26	College Humor	7
	Cosmopolitan		2 Science and Invention	24	Science and Invention	6
	Red Book		2 Judge	19	Popular Science	5
	Western Story		2 Western Story	13	Judge	4

Thus by comparing Tables XV and IX it is seen that out of the fourteen most popular magazines at the ages 12–13 eleven are common to the two lists; at the ages 14–16 eleven are common to the two lists; at the ages 14–16 eleven are

INVESTIGATIONS BY QUESTIONNAIRE 61

common; at the ages 17–18 ten are common. At the ages 12–13, for example, the boys of the present investigation read in addition to those common to the two lists, the *American Magazine*, *Red Book*, and *Western Story*, while those of the former investigation read in addition, *St. Nicholas*, *Boy Scout Magazine*, and *Ladies Home Journal*. It is thus seen that the likenesses are much more important than the differences.

Similar results also appear in the case of girls, a fact which the next table sets forth clearly.

TABLE XVI
Most Popular Magazines of Charlotte and Greensboro
Girls Points = sum of first, second, and third choices.

Age 12–14		14–16		17–18	
Number 99		568		197	
American	47	American	409	American	150
Ladies Home Journal	29	Ladies Home Journal	167	Literary Digest	72
McCall's	16	Cosmopolitan	135	Ladies Home Journal	66
Pictorial Review	16	Literary Digest	128	Cosmopolitan	48
Good Housekeeping	16	Good Housekeeping	111	Good Housekeeping	36
Cosmopolitan	13	Pictorial Review	107	Sat. Evening Post	31
St. Nicholas	13	Sat. Evening Post	92	McCall's	29
Literary Digest	12	McCall's	84	National Geographic	16
Sat. Evening Post	11	Photoplay	61	Red Book	16
Youth's Companion	11	National Geographic	59	Mentor	11
Photoplay	9	Red Book	51	Life	9
Woman's Home Comp	8	Woman's Home Comp	45	Review of Reviews	9
Delineator	7	True Story	38	Woman's Home Comp.	8
Judge	5	Life	37	Pictorial Review	7

Let us compare these results with Table IX, page 45, which sets forth the previous results. At the years 12–13 nine out of fourteen magazines are the same, at 14–16 nine are the same, at 17–18 ten are the same. The 12–13 year old girls of Charlotte and Greensboro prefer the *American*, *McCall's*, *Photoplay*, *Good Housekeeping*, and *Judge*, while those of the previous investigation like better the *Woman's World*, *American Boy*, *Life*, *Little Folks* and *Red Book*.

Similar differences occur at the other ages. In brief, in spite of the changes in locality and in time, the type of magazine interesting to girls has remained the same. There are, of course, certain differences between cities having similar conditions of education, wealth, and general culture. For example, during the years 12-13 nearly nine per cent of the boys in Charlotte say they do not like to read magazines well enough to enter all three choices while there are none in Greensboro. Greensboro High School has made much of its library for several years while Charlotte is just now developing hers. It is possible that there may be some connection between this fact of no choice and that of the excellence of the library. More boys and girls of Charlotte report at all ages that they do not like to read than do those of Greensboro. A larger percentage of the Charlotte boys like magazines of adventure and nature (due to the *National Geographic*), while a larger percentage of the Greensboro boys like magazines of science and humor. (This difference is quite large.) In the remaining groups the differences are small. The girls of Charlotte like nature (here again the *National Geographic*) and woman's arts, while those of Greensboro prefer humor. In the remaining types the results are quite similar. The twenty leading magazines (Table XVII) at each age group are quite similar, the one outstanding difference being the popularity of the *National Geographic* in Charlotte.

The detailed likenesses and differences between the two cities may be observed in the tables below which present the most popular magazines in each grade from each city. They are juxtaposed so that the differences may be clearly seen. In addition it seemed necessary to classify magazines in this way, since the grade is more nearly the school unit than the group of years. These tables will undoubtedly be of use for those desiring to know what good magazines are also interesting.

INVESTIGATIONS BY QUESTIONNAIRE 63

MOST POPULAR MAGAZINES OF GREENSBORO AND CHARLOTTE
ARRANGED BY GRADES (TABLES XVII AND XVIII)
Points = Sum of first, second, and third choices.
Grade VIII (*Boys*)

Greensboro		Charlotte	
Number 37		198	
Boys Life	18	American Boy	70
Popular Mechanics	14	American Magazine	52
American Boy	13	Boys Life	47
Popular Science	11	Literary Digest	42
American	9	Popular Mechanics	39
Life	6	Popular Science	39
Saturday Evening Post	4	National Geographic	35
Judge	4	Saturday Evening Post	33
Physical Culture	3	Science and Invention	18
True Story	3	Ladies Home Journal	12
Red Book	3	True Story	11
Colliers	2	Youth's Companion	11
Red Pepper	2	Western Story	10
Liberty	2	Life	8
Nature Study	2	Radio News	7
Youth's Companion	2	Country Gentleman	7
Adventure	1	Physical Review	7
Literary Digest	1	Physical Culture	6
Strength	1	McCalls	6
		Colliers	5

Greensboro		Grade IX	Charlotte	
Number 104			125	
American Magazine	53		American Boy	59
Boys Life	38		American Magazine	46
American Boy	32		Boys Life	33
Popular Science	22		Popular Mechanics	25
Popular Mechanics	22		Saturday Evening Post	24
Saturday Evening Post	16		National Geographic	19
Literary Digest	15		Literary Digest	16
Judge	10		Popular Science	16
Life	8		Red Book	15
Cosmopolitan	6		Cosmopolitan	9
Colliers	4		Photoplay	7
Western Story	3		College Humor	6
Red Pepper	3		Ladies Home Journal	5
National Geographic	3		Youth's Companion	4
Red Book	3		Short Story	3
Mentor	3		Judge	3
College Humor	3		True Detective Misteries	3
Whiz Bang	3		Science and Invention	3
Youth's Companion	2		Liberty	2
			Whiz Bang	2

64 CHILDREN'S INTERESTS IN READING

TABLE XVII (Continued)
Grade X (*Boys*)

Greensboro		Charlotte	
Number 54		70	
American Magazine	36	American Magazine	38
Literary Digest	13	American Boy	24
Life	15	Literaty Digest	17
Popular Science	12	Popular Mechanics	15
American Boy	12	Saturday Evening Post	12
Cosmopolitan	12	National Geographic	11
Saturday Evening Post	9	Cosmopolitan	11
Judge	7	Boys Life	9
Boys Life	5	Colliers	7
Collier's	4	Popular Science	6
Popular Mechanics	3	Life	4
True Story	3	Science and Invention	4
National Geographic	2	Liberty	4
Physical Culture	2	College Comics	3
Adventure	2	Red Book	3
College Humor	1	Field and Stream	3
Red Pepper	1	Wireless Age	2
Review of Reviews	1	Western Story	2
Baseball	1	Sport Story	2
		Mentor	2

Grade XI

Greensboro		Charlotte	
Number 61		45	
American Magazine	39	American Magazine	32
Literary Digest	21	Saturday Evening Post	17
Saturday Evening Post	15	Cosmopolitan	15
Popular Science	13	American Boy	12
National Geographic	10	Literary Digest	11
Life	10	Red Book	5
American Boy	9	Science and Invention	5
Popular Mechanics	9	College Humor	4
Boys Life	7	Life	3
College Humor	7	Radio News	2
Colliers	6	National Geographic	2
Cosmopolitan	3	Pictorial Review	2
Red Book	3	Colliers	2
Judge	3	Youth's Companion	2
True Story	2	Boys Life	1
Mentor	2	Architectural Record	1
Red Pepper	1	Current History	1

INVESTIGATIONS BY QUESTIONNAIRE 65

Youth's Companion	1	Mentor	1
Wireless Age	1	Love Stories	1
Baseball	1	Popular Mechanics	1

TABLE XVIII
Grade VIII (*Girls*)

Greensboro		Charlotte	
Number 66		196	
American Magazine	43	American Magazine	94
Literary Digest	16	Ladies Home Journal	57
Pictorial Review	15	Pictorial Review	35
Life	12	McCalls	34
Good Housekeeping	11	True Story	33
Cosmopolitan	10	Cosmopolitan	31
Popular Science	9	Good Housekeeping	36
Ladies Home Journal	9	National Geographic	26
Woman's Home Companion	5	Literary Digest	25
Photoplay	5	Photoplay	20
Red Book	5	Red Book	16
Youth's Companion	4	Saturday Evening Post	15
American Girl	4	Youth's Companion	14
McCalls	4	St. Nicholas	13
Saturday Evening Post	3	Delineator	9
Judge	2	Motion Picture	9
St. Nicholas	2	Colliers	8
Boys Life	2	True Romance	8
Mentor	2	Love Stories	8
True Story	2	Woman's Home Companion	8

Grade IX

Greensboro		Charlotte	
Number 147		175	
American Magazine	95	American Magazine	95
Ladies Home Journal	34	Ladies Home Journal	59
Woman's Home Companion	38	Cosmopolitan	34
Pictorial Review	25	McCalls	32
Photoplay	23	Pictorial Review	27
Literary Digest	21	Good Housekeeping	27
Good Housekeeping	20	Saturday Evening Post	25
McCalls	18	National Geographic	21
Saturday Evening Post	16	Literary Digest	16
College Humor	11	Red Book	15
Red Book	9	Woman's Home Companion	10
Colliers	8	Hearst's International	9
National Geographic	7	Photoplay	6

66   CHILDREN'S INTERESTS IN READING

Judge	7	St. Nicholas	6
Life	7	True Story	4
True Story	6	College Humor	4
Physical Culture	5	Colliers	4
St. Nicholas	4	Youth's Companion	3
American Girl	4	Delineator	3
		Popular Science	3

TABLE XVIII (Continued)
Grade X   (*Girls*)

Greensboro		Charlotte	
Number 91		105	
American Magazine	70	American Magazine	60
Cosmopolitan	21	Cosmopolitan	29
Literary Digest	20	Literary Digest	25
Saturday Evening Post	16	Good Housekeeping	23
Ladies Home Journal	15	Saturday Evening Post	18
Good Housekeeping	15	Pictorial Review	15
Pictorial Review	13	McCalls	13
Life	11	National Geographic	10
McCalls	11	Woman's Home Companion	9
Photoplay	10	Red Book	9
Judge	6	Photoplay	6
Red Book	5	Life	6
College Humor	5	Youth's Companion	4
Woman's Home Companion	4	Delineator	4
National Geographic	4	Colliers	3
Atlantic Monthly	4	Sport Stories	3
McCalls	3	College Humor	2
Youth's Companion	3	Review of Reviews	2
True Story	3	Hearst's International	2
Popular Science	3		

Grade XI

Greensboro		Charlotte	
Number 90		99	
American Magazine	71	American Magazine	75
Literary Digest	43	Literary Digest	42
Mentor	19	Cosmopolitan	34
Ladies Home Journal	18	Saturday Evening Post	30
Life	16	Ladies Home Journal	26
Good Housekeeping	15	Good Housekeeping	24
Saturday Evening Post	13	Woman's Home Companion	16
National Geographic	10	McCalls	10
Cosmopolitan	9	Red Book	8
Woman's Home Companion	6	National Geographic	7

INVESTIGATIONS BY QUESTIONNAIRE 67

Judge	4	World's Work	6	
Atlantic	4	Pictorial Review	4	
McCall's	4	Youth's Companion	4	
Photoplay	3	Etude	3	
College Humor	3	Review of Reviews	3	
Time	2	Atlantic	3	
Youth's Companion	2	True Story	2	
Red Book	2	Delineator	2	
Hearst's International	2	The Classic	2	
Golden Book	2	College Humor	2	

From these tables it seems clear that between any two corresponding grades there are five or six magazines in which there is general agreement but when these are taken out the remaining choices are more scattering. At times the smallness of the numbers of pupils choosing makes it possible for a magazine to be included which would not be the case were there a larger number choosing. As more and more data are collected these unusual choices drop out and more similarity results. Thus the results are just as similar when comparisons are made over a period of years as between two corresponding grades of two cities less than a hundred miles apart when the census was taken during the same month. There are, for example, among the boys in the eighth grade only eleven out of twenty magazines the same; in the ninth, fourteen; in the tenth, thirteen; and in the eleventh, thirteen. A similar condition exists among the girls, for the corresponding figures here are, for grade VIII, fourteen; for Grade IX, fifteen, for grade X, fifteen; and for grade XI, thirteen. Of course when we think of the hundreds of magazines which might have been chosen the most striking characteristic of the findings may be considered to be the large number which are alike, i.e. the fact that eleven out of twenty are alike is a striking example of the similarity in interest in corresponding grades in adjacent cities.

In general there are remarkable likenesses between types of magazines chosen in adjacent cities and from time to time. Boys choose more widely magazines dealing with adventure and daring, with the great machines of the day, and with humor. Fiction appeals to both boys and girls, but the latter choose more of it. Girls like best magazines concerned with woman's arts in which there is a plenteous sprinkling of love stories. They read only a little humor and few if any magazines of a scientific nature. They like those that show pictures of the latest styles. The *American Magazine* is probably the most popular magazine among both boys and girls of high school age.

Books

The books which the high school pupils of these two cities listed were classified into the same categories which were used on the former occasion. Indeed the same person[1] classified the books in both cases, so that the results are comparable. Careful records were kept of the number of boys and girls who do not like to read books. In this way Table XIX was arrived at. Here, it will be noted, the results obtained from both cities were combined.

Table XIX
Percentage Table Indicating the Relative Proportion of Books Chosen in Each Class. Greensboro and Charlotte.

Number	B	75	471	151
	G	98	664	184
Age		*12–13*	*14–16*	*17–18*
Adult Fiction	B	11.2	13.8	24.2
	G	35.1	48.6	56.9
Juvenile Fiction	B	2.6	2.5	1.9
	G	38.9	17.6	9.2
Adventure	B	61.6	63.3	52.8
	G	20.2	25.4	26.6
Biography	B	2.6	2.3	1.3
	G	.6	.8	1.0
History	B	2.3	.5	.1
	G	..	..	..

[1] Carrie Nicholson Jordan.

Poetry	B	.5	1.2	3.0
	G	..	1.6	2.1
Science	B	..	.1	.1
	G	..	.1	.1
Travel	B	..	.1	.1
	G	..	..	..
Information	B	.5	.6	.6
	G	.2	..	..
Humor	B	9.4	7.3	7.5
	G	2.5	3.3	1.9
Miscellaneous	B	.3	.1	.1
	G	.4	..	..
No Choice	B	6.5	8.1	7.9
	G	3.5	3.2	1.7
Total Percent	B	100	100	100
	G	100	100	100

The number choosing the various types of books is immediately seen. Boys like adventure above everything else. Think of it, more than 50 per cent of the books listed by them are classified as adventure. Fiction, too, claims a considerable share of interest with an initial percentage of 11 and a final one of 24. Humor comes next with 7 to 10 per cent, depending on the age. Possibly this large amount is due to the inclusion in this group of *Tom Sawyer* and *Huckleberry Finn*. Juvenile fiction, history, and biography seem to have a very slight appeal among boys, while science, travel, and information hardly count among books interesting.

Certain changes of interest are worth noticing. Fiction beginning with 11 per cent at the ages 12–13 has more than doubled by the time years 17–18 are reached. The greatest increase comes between the age group 14–16 and 17–18. The interest in adventure, so large at first gives way somewhat to the interest in fiction during the years 17–18. While history and biography become less interesting, poetry becomes more so; although at best this interest is not very great. The number of boys who left out the names of some of the five books increases slightly during the high school period.

Girls like fiction best of all. For example, during the years 12–13, seventy-four per cent of all books are either adult or juvenile fiction and this is representative of all age groups. They show, too, a substantial interest in books of adventure giving many votes to books like *Treasure Island* and *The Call of the Wild*, and to others of a similar nature. Books of humor claim only a small share—2 to 3 per cent—of their attention. As for the others, history, biography, science, travel, and information, very few are chosen. And finally, two per cent of the books are poetry at the year 17–18. The number of girls not preferring any books is small.

Do the interests of girls change from year to year? In two cases—fiction and adventure—there are striking changes: (1) fiction increases from 35 to 57 per cent during the years 12–18; (2) adventure increases from 20 to 27 per cent during this same period. On the contrary juvenile fiction decreases rapidly from about 39 per cent at years 12–13 to 9 per cent during the years 17–18. Humor increases slightly during the years 14–16, but decreases during the next group of years. The number of pupils not choosing books of any sort decreases as the years increase.

Differences in interest between boys and girls there are a plenty. From two to three times as many books of adventure are chosen by boys as by girls. In fiction a similar difference appears though in the opposite direction for, from two to three times as many girls as boys prefer this type. The difference is greatest during the years 14–16 although it is only slightly greater than at the ages 12–13. Juvenile fiction, too, furnishes another great difference, possibly the greatest, between these two groups. Fourteen times as many girls as boys choose this type of book during the years 12–13, and these differences continue during the years 14-18. Biography and history are seldom chosen. No girls seem to like books of travel and information, and only a few boys do. Boys certainly do read more books of humor than do girls, for nine books of this type are chosen by boys to two or three by girls. Finally, girls like to read better than boys, especially is this true at the years 17-18 as here nearly eight per cent of the boys do not like to read books, while less than two per cent of the girls have no predilections in this direction.

Let us now consider the differences in types of books chosen by boys and girls in 1917 in municipalities like Washington, D. C., and Fayetteville, Arkansas, with those chosen eight years later in Charlotte and Greensboro, cities of North Carolina. Two tables, XIX and XX, set forth the percentage of each type chosen during the two investigations. Boys might be first considered. In adult fiction the differences are small indeed; the first investigation shows fewer choices during the years 12-13 (six and eleven) and a somewhat larger number during the years 17-18 than the second. Adventure is so much alike that it seems almost beyond belief. The first investigation shows a much larger per cent of boys reading juvenile fiction than does the second one, for during the years 12-13, nineteen per cent preferred juvenile fiction in the first investigation, while about three per cent chose it in the second. This fact may have been due to the inclusion of some of the seventh grade boys in the first investigation. The same difference is shown in the upper grades. There is little, if any, difference in interest in the case of biography, history, poetry, science, travel, and information. A little over twice as many boys of the second investigation chose magazines of humor than did those of the first. And finally more than twice as many blank spaces appear instead of books in the second investigation.

The similarities between the girls concerned in the former and present investigations are marked. In fiction no closer correlation could have been anticipated. In juvenile fiction

TABLE XX
PERCENTAGE TABLE INDICATING THE RELATIVE PROPORTION OF BOOKS CHOSEN IN EACH CLASS. (105 PUPILS AGES 19–23 OMITTED IN THIS TABLE)

		1917			
Boys		59	253	846	283
Girls		87	336	1195	414
Age		*9–11*	*12–13*	*14–16*	*17–18*
Adult Fiction	B.	4	6	18	30
	G.	15	33	45	58
Juvenile Fiction	B.	27	19	11	9
	G.	67	44	30	13
Adventure	B.	56	64	59	49
	G.	12	17	18	22
Biography	B.	3	2	1	1
	G.	...	...	1	1
History	B.	1	1	1	...
	G.	...	...	...	...
Poetry	B.	...	1	1	1
	G.	...	1	2	6
Science	B.	...	1	...	...
	G.	...	...	...	...
Travel	B.	...	...	...	...
	G.	...	...	...	...
Information	B.	4	2	...	...
	G.	1	...	...	...
Humor	B.	1	3	5	4
	G.	1	2	...	1
Miscellaneous	B.	...	...	2	1
	G.	1	...	...	...
No Choice	B.	4	1	4	5
	G.	3	3	2	2
Total	B.	100	100	100	100
	G.	100	100	100	100

the interest is greater in the former study than in this one. This shows up especially well in the age group 14–16. Slightly more girls of the more recent census chose books of adventure and humor. The two groups are alike in number of books chosen concerning biography, history, science, travel, information, and no choices—while a few more of the first group chose poetry.

In general it seems clear that the same types of books, almost the same proportions, were chosen in the second as in the first study. The type of book, then, remains very constant over a period of eight years.

Comparison between the Charlotte High School and the Greensboro High School concerning their choices of books is valuable. Greensboro boys like fiction much better than do those of Charlotte. This difference is greatest during the years 12-13. If the per cents for the three age groups are added the boys of Greensboro give fiction 61 points while those of Charlotte give it 44. In adventure, though the differences are slight, still from 6 to 10 per cent more boys in Charlotte vote for this. In biography, history, juvenile fiction, poetry, science, travel, information, humor, and no choice, the differences are indeed slight.

The girls of these two localities also show great similarities in interests in books. The per cent choosing books of fiction, juvenile, fiction and adventure are very nearly the same. They are alike in not choosing history, science, travel, and information. There are some slight differences in poetry since 4 per cent of the girls of Greensboro at the age of 12-13 say they like poetry while there are practically none in Charlotte. All through the high school this difference in interest in poetry persists. Again the girls of Charlotte during the years 17-18 say they like adventure better than do those of Greensboro. But despite these discrepancies there is altogether a remarkable similarity between these two cities in the type of book chosen by high school pupils. In answer to our query concerning the similarity of choices between nearby cities we find that the relation is remarkably close. Moreover, Tables XXI and XXII set forth a list of most popular books for each city arranged by age groups.

CHILDREN'S INTERESTS IN READING

MOST POPULAR BOOKS
TABLE XXI
Boys Greensboro
Points = Sum of first, second, third, fourth, and fifth choices.

Number 64		Number 152		Number 66	
Age 12–13		Age 14–16		Age 17–18	
Zane Gray's Books	16	Zane Gray's Books	106	Zane Gray	32
Tom Sawyer	5	Call of the Wild	36	Ben Hur	8
Huckleberry Finn	4	Covered Wagon	34	The Spy	8
Treasure Island	4	Tarzan Series	32	Huckleberry Finn	6
Call of the Wild	3	Tom Sawyer	22	O. Henry Stories	6
The Spy	3	Huckleberry Finn	19	Sea Hawk	6
Kidnapped	2	Treasure Island	17	Tom Sawyer	5
Penrod	2	O'Henry Stories	11	Call of the Wild	5
Last of the Mochicans	2	Ben Hur	11	Tarzan Series	4
Captains Courageous	2	Three Musketeers	10	Last of the Mochicans	4
Bob, Son of Battle	2	HighSchoolBoysSeries	10	Mark Twain Books	4
Gods of Mars	2	Man without a Country	8	Seventeen	2
		Baseball Jo Series	7	Three Musketeers	2
		Tom Swift Series	6	House of Seven Gables	2
		Virginian	6	Scottish Chiefs	2
		The Spy	5	Laddie	2
		White Fang	5	Covered Wagon	2
		Circus Boy Series	5	Spell of the Yukon	2
		Oliver Twist	4	Golden Snake	2
		Ivanhoe	4	Irving's Stories	2
		Boy Scout Series	4	David Copperfield	2
		Last of the Mohicans	3		
		Oregon Trail	3		
		Life of O'Henry	3		

Girls

Number 28		Number 280		Number 84	
Age 12–13		Age 14–16		Age 17–18	
Nobody's Boy and Girl	7	Zane Gray's Books	68	O. Henry Stories	15
Zane Gray's Books	6	O. Henry	38	Little Women	13
Treasure Island	3	To Have and to Hold	28	Little Minister	8
Four Millions	3	Little Women	25	Lorna Doone	8
Ben Hur	3	Seventeen	25	David Copperfield	7
		Ben Hur	21	So Big	7
		Scaramouche	20	Rivals	7
		Girl of the Limber-Lost	19	Ben Hur	6
				Zane Gray's Books	6

INVESTIGATIONS BY QUESTIONNAIRE 75

Secret Garden	19	Last of the Mohicans	6
Little Minister	19	Mill on the Floss	6
Trail of the Lonesome Pine	18	Covered Wagon	5
		To Have and to Hold	5
Anne of Green Gables	17	Trail of the Lonesome Pine	5
So Big	17		
Freckles	17	Girl of the Limberlost	4
Covered Wagon	16		
Call of the Wild	16	Ben Hur	4
Tale of Two Cities	15	Virginian	4
Three Musketeers	14	Laddie	4
Tom Sawyer	13	Shepherd of the Hills	4
Virginian	12	Tale of Two Cities	4
Ivanhoe	11	Ivanhoe	4
Lorna Doone	11	Silas Marner	4
The Sheik	11	Freckles	4
		Shakespeare's Works	4
		Jane Eyre	4

TABLE XXII

Boys		Charlotte			
Number 52		149		85	
Age 12–13		14–16		17–18	
Zane Gray's Works	22	Zane Gray's Works	291	Zane Gray's Works	84
Call of the Wild	16	Call of the Wild	71	Ivanhoe	22
Tom Swift Series	14	Treasure Island	68	Treasure Island	18
Treasure Island	11	Tom Sawyer	67	Huckleberry Finn	16
Huckleberry Finn	9	Tarzan Series	46	Tom Swift Series	11
Tarzan Series	7	Tom Swift Series	45	When a Man's a Man	8
Driven from Home	6	Penrod	40	Tarzan	6
Boy Scout Series	6	Last of the Mohicans	37	Laddie	6
Rover Boy Series	6	Rover Boy Series	21	Rivers End	5
Penrod	5	Sea Hawk	13	Last of the Mohicans	5
Last of the Mohicans	4	Robinson Crusoe	12	Sea Hawk	4
Kazan	4	Kazan	11	Seventeen	2
Robin Hood	4	Prince and Pauper	9	Penrod	2
Radio Boy Series	3	Covered Wagon	8	Robinson Crusoe	2
Tom Sawyer	2	Mark Twain's Works	8	Kazan	2
Covered Wagon	2	Robin Hood	7	That Printer of Udell's	2
Kidnapped	2	Ivanhoe	7		
To have and to Hold	2	Boy Ally Series	7	Nomads of the North	2
Sentimental Tommy	2	Oliver Twist	6	Gods of Mars	2
Buffalo Bill	2	Hiawatha	6	Kidnapped	2

Children's Interests in Reading

Tom Slade Series	2	Seventeen	6	Tale of Two Cities	2
Sea Hawk	2	Buffalo Bill and the		David Copperfield	2
Winning of Barbara		Pony Express	5	Sherlock Holmes	2
Worth	2	Laddie	5	The Flirt	2
Arabian Nights	2	White Fang	5	Little Shepherd of	
Ruggles of Red Gap	2			Kingdom Come	2
Roy Blakeley	2				
Sink or Swim	2				
Billy Whiskers	2				

		Girls Charlotte			
Number 70		385		100	
Age 12–13		*14–16*		*17–18*	
Zane Gray's Works	18	Zane Gray's Works	183	Zane Gray's Works	65
Girl of the Limberlost	15	Girl of the Limberlost	107	Girl of the Limberlost	27
Little Women	13	Little Women	51	Anne of Green Gables	16
Little Colonel		Anne of Green Gables	50	Little Shepherd of	
Series	9	Pollyanna	48	Kingdom Come	11
Pollyanna	8	Graustark	40	Her Father's Daughter	8
Last of the Mohicans	8	Freckles	35	Tale of Two Cities	8
Secret Garden	7	Laddie	34	Treasure Island	8
Heidi	7	Little Shepherd of		Graustark	7
Seventeen	6	Kingdom Come	33	Little Minister	6
Rebecca of Sunny-		Last of the Mohicans	29	Seventeen	5
brook Farm	6	Ivanhoe	25	Secret Garden	5
Mrs. Wiggs of the		Silas Marner	24	Twice Told Tales	5
Cabbage Patch	5	Tale of Two Cities	23	Rosary	5
Freckles	5	Treasure Island	23	Circular Staircase	5
Laddie	5	Huckleberry Finn	19	Freckles	5
Polly Series	5	Seventeen	18	Life of Helen Keller	4
Elsie Dinsmore	4	Rebecca of Sunny-		Tom Sawyer	4
Patty Series	4	brook Farm	16	Red Rock	4
Rose in Bloom	4	Harvester	16	Jane Eyre	4
Janice Meredith	4	David Copperfield	15	Top of the World	4
Graustark Series	3	Penrod	14	Treasure Island	3
Tom Sawyer	3	Covered Wagon	14	Freckles	3
Penrod		Little Women	12	Ben Hur	3
Freckles	3	When a Man's a Man	11	Sea Hawk	3
Ivanhoe	3	When Knighthood was		Laddie	3
Little Minister	3	in Flower	11		
Anne of Avonlea	3	Oliver Twist	11		
House of Seven Gables	3				
Spy	3				

INVESTIGATIONS BY QUESTIONNAIRE 77

Most Popular Books Arranged by Ages Charlotte and Greensboro

TABLE XXIII

Boys Points = Sum of first, second, third, fourth, and fifth choices.

Number 58		301		151	
Age 12–13		14–16		17–18	
Zane Gray's Works	38	Zane Gray's Works	397	Zane Gray's Works	116
Call of the Wild	19	Call of the Wild	107	Ivanhoe	22
Tom Swift Series	14	Tom Sawyer	89	Huckleberry Finn	22
Huckleberry Finn	13	Treasure Island	85	Treasure Island	18
Treasure Island	11	Tarzan Series	78	Tom Swift Series	11
Penrod	7	Tom Swift Series	51	Sea Hawk	10
Tom Sawyer	7	Covered Wagon	42	Tarzan Series	10
Tarzan Series	7	Penrod	40	When a Man's a Man	8
Driven from Home	6	Last of the Mohicans	40	Ben Hur	8
Boy Scout Series	6	Rover Boy Series	20	Spy	8
Rover Boy Series	6	Sea Hawk	13	Last of the Mohicans	7
Last of the Mohicans	6	Robinson Crusoe	12	Laddie	6
Kidnapped	4	Kazan	11	O. Henry Stories	6
Kazan	4	O. Henry Stories	11	River's End	5
Robin Hood	4	Ben Hur	11	Tom Sawyer	5
Radio Boy Series	3	Oliver Twist	10	Call of the Wild	5
The Spy	3	White Fang	10	Seventeen	4
Tom Slade Series	2	Three Musketeers	10	Mark Twain's Books	4
Covered Wagon	2	High School Boys		David Copperfield	4
Sentimental Tommy	2	Series	10	Penrod	2
Buffalo Bill	2	Prince and Pauper	9	Robinson Crusoe	2
Sea Hawk	2	Mark Twain's Books	8	Kazan	2
Winning of Barbara		Man without a Country	8	That Printer of	
Worth	2	Robin Hood	7	Udell's	2
To Have and to Hold	2	Ivanhoe	7	Nomads of the North	2
Arabian Nights	2	Boy Ally Series	7	Gods of Mars	2
Ruggles of Red Gap	2			Kidnapped	2

TABLE XXIV

Girls Points = Sum of first, second, third, fourth, and fifth choices.

Number 98		665		251	
Age 12–13		14–16		17–18	
Zane Gray's Works	24	Zane Gray's Works	252	Zane Gray's Works	71
Girl of the		Girl of the		Girl of the	
Limberlost	15	Limberlost	126	Limberlost	31
Little Women	13	Little Women	88	O. Henry Stories	17
Little Colonel Series	9	Anne of Green Gables	67	Anne of Green	
Last of the Mohicans	8	Freckles	53	Gables	16
Pollyanna	8	Pollyanna	52	Little Minister	14

Secret Garden	7	Little Shepherd of		Little Women	13
Heidi	7	Kingdom Come	42	Tale of Two Cities	12
When Knighthood was		Graustark Series	42	Little Shepherd of	
in Flower	7	O. Henry Stories	40	Kingdom Come	11
Seventeen	6	Laddie	38	David Copperfield	10
Rebecca of Sunnybook		Seventeen	32	Ben Hur	9
Farm	6	To have and to Hold	32	Lorna Doone	8
Mrs. Wiggs of the		Silas Marner	31	Her Father's	
Cabbage Patch	5	Covered Wagon	30	Daughter	8
Freckles	5	Tale of Two Cities	27	Treasure Island	8
Laddie	5	Scaramouche	26	Jane Eyre	8
Eight Cousins	5	David Copperfield	24	So Big	7
Polly Series	4	Treasure Island	23	Graustark Series	7
Elsie Dinsmore	4	Huckleberry Finn	19	The Rivals	7
Patty Series	4	Virginian	18	Last of the Mohicans	6
Rose in Bloom	4	Penrod	17	Mill on the Floss	6
Janice Meredith	4	Harvester	16	Pollyanna	6
Graustark Series	3	Three Musketeers	14	Freckles	5
Tom Sawyer	3	When Knighthood was		Covered Wagon	5
Mammy's White Folks	3	in Flower	11	To Have and to Hold	5
Penrod	3			Trail of the Lone-	
Fairy Tales	3			some Pine	5
				Tom Sawyer	4

Tables XXIII and VIII set forth at each age group a list of the most popular books which were selected by boys in the first study and in the second. Twenty books are listed from each study at each age. Of these twenty at the ages 12-13 seven are alike; at the ages 14-16 six; and at the ages 17-18, seven. Probably the greatest difference is the modern interest in Zane Gray's works since it has displaced *The Call of the Wild* as the most popular book at nearly all ages. The choices in the previous investigation seem somewhat more immature in including as they do *Black Beauty*, *Little Men*, and *Little Women*. One notes also some other recent books in the popular lists such as *The Covered Wagon*, *Kazan*, and the High School Boy Series. It seems that Tom Swift Series and the Rover Boy Series have displaced the Motor Boy Series. During the years 17-18 several books such as Zane Grays works, Tom Swift Series, *The Sea Hawk*, and the

Tarzan Series are added, while *The Tale of Two Cities, The Trail of the Lonesome Pine, David Copperfield, Lorna Doone,* and *Freckles* are left out. On the other hand *Huckleberry Finn, Tom Sawyer, Treasure Island, The Call of the Wild,* and *Penrod* retain their popularity. They appear at all ages and are undoubtedly very interesting to young people at 12-18 years.

Table XXIV shows similarly, the books most frequently chosen by girls. Here the likeness is more striking than it was among the boys, for from eight to nine books are alike in each age group. *Pollyanna, Freckles, The Girl of the Limberlost,* and *Little Women* are still popular at all times, while *Rebecca of Sunnybrook Farm, Laddie* and the Little Colonel Series are popular at the ages of 12-13. On the other hand Zane Gray's works in the second investigation lead all the rest by good majorities at every age group. O. Henry's stories appear on the popularity lists largely because of Greensboro, the birthplace of O. Henry, a city which has commemorated the name of this gifted writer by calling attention to his works in a wide variety of ways such as by naming its leading hotel for him. Some of the newer books appearing during the ages 14-16 have been played in the motion pictures. Again, during the years 17-18 there are nine books alike in the two lists. Aside from Zane Gray's works the lists are much alike. To get then a clear understanding of the sort of things that girls like during the high school period, take one of Zane Gray's books, *The Girl of the Limberlost, Little Women, Little Shepherd of Kingdom Come,* or *Freckles* and read them.

It would seem therefore that while the type of book liked by both boys and girls was very nearly the same in the two investigations, the actual books change. Of course there are many which remain popular from time to time, but the high school pupil's fancy is caught by the book of the hour attracting his attention as it does, not only by its display in advantageous positions in store windows but also in motion pictures.

And finally, as far as general discussion goes, it was thought important to arrange the twenty most popular books by grades rather than by ages (Tables XXV and XXVI), and to tabulate the percentage of each type appearing at each grade (Table XXVII). There is no great difference here between this arrangement and the previous one by ages except that it may be a little more convenient for reference.

Most Popular Books Arranged by Grades
Charlotte and Greensboro

Table XXV

Points = Sum of first, second, third, fourth, and fifth choices.

Boys

Number	239		237	
Grade	VIII		IX	
Zane Gray's Works	187	Zane Gray's Works	208
Call of the Wild	59	Call of the Wild	52
Tom Sawyer	59	Covered Wagon	35
Treasure Island	54	Huckleberry Finn	30
Tom Swift Series	46	Treasure Island	29
Tarzan Series	44	Tarzan Series	29
Huckleberry Finn	43	Tom Swift Series	23
Penrod	33	Last of the Mohicans	14
Last of the Mohicans	28	Ben Hur	10
Boy Scout Series	17	Tom Sawyer	10
Kazan	15	High School Boy Series	9
Robin Hood	11	Rover Boy Series	8
Sea Hawk	8	Baseball Jo Series	7
Robinson Crusoe	7	Sea Hawk	5
Driven from Home	6	White Fang	5
Hiawatha	6	The Spy	5
Seventeen	6	Circus Boy Series	5
Prince and Pauper	6	Robinson Crusoe	5
Sherlock Holmes	5	Kidnapped	4
Boy Ally Series	5	Boy Scout Series	4

INVESTIGATIONS BY QUESTIONNAIRE 81

Number	118		103	
Grade	X		XI	
Zane Gray's Works		84	Zane Gray's Works	72
Call of the Wild		21	Huckleberry Finn	17
Tarzan Series		18	Tom Sawyer	14
Treasure Island		17	Ivanhoe	14
Huckleberry Finn		13	Treasure Island	13
Oliver Twist		13	O. Henry Stories	11
Sea Hawk		12	Mark Twain	10
Ivanhoe		12	Laddie	8
When a Man' a Man		8	River's End	7
Tom Sawyer		7	Sea Hawk	6
Ben Hur		7	Call of the Wild	5
Three Musketeers		7	David Copperfield	4
Last of the Mohicans		7	Tarzan Series	4
Mark Twain's Works		5	Ben Hur	4
Virginian		4	Last of the Mohicans	4
Spy		4	Golden Snake	4
Seventeen		4	Spell of the Yukon	4
Captain Blood		3	Oliver Twist	4
Covered Wagon		3	Spy	4
Life of O. Henry		3	Scaramouche	3

TABLE XXVI
MOST POPULAR BOOKS ARRANGED BY GRADES
CHARLOTTE AND GREENSBORO

Points = Sum of first, second, third, fourth, and fifth choices.

Number	274		*Girls*	298	
Grade	VIII			IX	
Zane Gray's Works		83	Zane Gray's Works		112
Girl of the Limberlost		47	Girl of the Limberlost		65
Little Women		34	Little Women		52
Anne of Green Gables		32	Freckles		49
Secret Garden		26	Graustark Series		41
Pollyanna		24	Little Shepherd of		
Last of the Mohicans		21	Kingdom Come		37
Little Colonel Series		21	O. Henry Stories		25
Seventeen		16	Covered Wagon		24
Freckles		16	Tom Sawyer		21
Laddie		15	Anne of Green Gables		20
Rebecca of Sunnybrook Farm		12	To Have and to Hold		18
Little Men		12	Rebecca of Sunnybrook Farm		16
Anne of Avonlea		12	Trail of the Lonesome Pine		14
Huckleberry Finn		11	Harvester		14
Polly Series		10	Tarzan Series		13

Elsie Dinsmore	10	Tale of Two Cities	12
Heidi	10	Mammy's White Folks	11
Graustark Series	10	Scaramouche	11
Penrod	9	The Sheik	11
		Freckles	10

Number	194		182	
Grade	X		XI	
Zane Gray's Works	69	Zane Gray's Works	62
Girl of the Limberlost	41	O. Henry Stories	32
Little Minister	26	Tale of Two Cities	21
Tale of Two Cities	24	Ivanhoe	20
Silas Marner	22	Ben Hur	18
Anne of Green Gables	21	Girl of the Limberlost	16
Laddie	15	So Big	13
Three Musketeers	14	Lorna Doone	13
Graustark Series	12	Little Women	13
Virginian	12	David Copperfield	11
Ivanhoe	11	To Have and to Hold	9
Rosary	11	Graustark Series	9
Seventeen	9	Treasure Island	8
Scaramouche	9	Rosary	8
Call of the Wild	8	Freckles	8
Girl Scout Series	8	Secret Garden	7
Little Women	7	Circular Staircase	7
Secret Garden	7	Silas Marner	7
Her Father's Daughter	7	Jane Eyre	7
Treasure Island	7	Silas Marner	7

TABLE XXVII
PERCENTAGE TABLE INDICATING THE RELATIVE PROPORTION OF BOOKS CHOSEN IN EACH CLASS ARRANGED BY GRADES
CHARLOTTE AND GREENSBORO

Number		239	244	120	105
	G	260	311	194	182
Grades		VIII	IX	X	XI
Adult Fiction	B	10.2	14.2	22.7	25.0
	G	37.5	44.9	57.3	56.9
Juvenile Fiction	B	3.5	2.4	1.7	.8
	G	31.7	15.4	9.7	9.3
Adventure	B	64.8	63.9	59.3	50.8
	G	21.0	25.6	26.6	26.0
Biography	B	2.0	1.3	3.7	2.5
	G	.6	1.0	.5	.9

INVESTIGATIONS BY QUESTIONNAIRE

History	B	.5	.7	....	.8
	G	.1	....	....	....
Poetry	B	1.1	.8	1.3	2.9
	G	.8	.8	2.2	2.6
Science	B	.1	....	.3	....
	G	....	....	....	.1
Travel	B	....	.2	....	.6
	G	.1	....	....	....
Information	B	.5	.6	.3	.4
	G	.1	....	....	....
Humor	B	9.6	6.2	6.4	7.5
	G	4.3	2.5	2.1	2.2
Miscellaneous	B	.2	.1	.2	.2
	G	.2	.1	....	....
No Choice	B	7.3	9.4	4.5	8.6
	G	3.6	3.2	1.8	2.0
Total	B	100	100	100	100
	G	100	100	100	100

Reference has already been made to the similarities and differences between Charlotte and Greensboro in respect to the general types of books preferred. We come now to a listing in parallel of the most popular books in each grade (Tables XXVIII, XXIX, XXX and XXXI). Among boys the most striking occurrence is that Zane Gray's works which, like Abou Ben Adhem's name, lead all the rest in every grade in both cities. I suppose that this series catches the interest of at least thirty per cent of the boys and probably more. *The Call of the Wild* no longer leads, but it does appear in every grade in many cases next to Zane Gray. *Huckleberry Finn* is another of those books, popular in all grades.

TABLE XXVIII
MOST POPULAR BOOKS. GREENSBORO
Points = sum of first, second, third, fourth, and fifth choices.
Boys

Number	37		109	
Grade	VIII		IX	
Zane Gray's Books		29	Zane Gray's Books	71
Tom Sawyer		12	Covered Wagon	24
Treasure Island		10	Tarzan Series	20

Call of the Wild	8	Call of the Wild	18
Tarzan Series	7	Huckleberry Finn	13
Three Musketeers	5	Ben Hur	10
Huckleberry Finn	5	High School Boys Series	9
Man without a Country	4	Baseball Jo Series	7
Virginian	2	Tom Swift Series	6
Boy Scout Series	2	Sea Hawk	5
High School Boys Series	2	White Fang	5
Keeper of the Bees	2	The Spy	5
		Circus Boy	5
		David Copperfield	4
		Boy Scout Series	4
		Man without a Country	4
		Ivanhoe	4
		The Spy	3
		Mine with the Iron Door	2
		O. Henry	2
Number	50		59
Grade	X		XI
Zane Gray's Works	22	Zane Gray's Works	32
Call of the Wild	15	O. Henry Short Stories	11
Three Musketeers	7	Huckleberry Finn	8
Tarzan Series	7	Tom Sawyer	5
Sea Hawk	5	Ben Hur	4
Ben Hur	5	Sea Hawk	4
Virginian	4	Last of the Mohicans	4
Spy	4	Golden Snake	4
Seventeen	4	Spell of the Yukon	4
Huckleberry Finn	3	Oliver Twist	4
Life of O. Henry	3	Mark Twain	4
Last of the Mohicans	3	Spy	4
Oliver Twist	4	Treasure Island	4
Jim Davis	2	Scaramouche	3
Tale of Two Cities	2	54-40 or Fight	3
Amateur Gentleman	2	Call of the Wild	3
Lost on the Moon	2	To Have and to Hold	2
House of Seven Gables	2	Tarzan Series	2
Captain Blood	2	David Copperfield	2
		Laddie	2

Table XXIX
Most Popular Books. Charlotte

Points = Sum of first, second, third, fourth, and fifth choices.

Number	202	*Boys*	128	
Grade	VIII	Points	IX	Points
Zane Gray's Works		158	Zane Gray's Works	137
Call of the Wild		51	Call of the Wild	34
Tom Sawyer		47	Treasure Island	29
Tom Swift Series		46	Tom Swift Series	17
Treasure Island		44	Huckleberry Finn	17
Huckleberry Finn		38	Last of the Mohicans	14
Tarzan Series		37	Covered Wagon	11
Penrod		33	Tom Sawyer	10
Last of the Mohicans		28	Tarzan Series	9
Kazan Series		15	Rover Boy Series	8
Boy Scout Series		15	Robinson Crusoe	5
Robin Hood		11	Kidnapped	4
Sea Hawk		8	God's Country and Woman	4
Robinson Crusoe		7	Prince and Pauper	3
Driven from Home		6	White Fang	3
Hiawatha		6	Laddie	3
Seventeen		6	Boy Scout Series	3
Prince and the Pauper		6	Mark Tidd Series	2
Sherlock Holmes		5	Boy Ally Series	2
Boy Ally Series		5	Courage of Captain Plumb	2

Number	68		44	
Grade	X		XI	
Zane Gray's Works		62	Zane Gray's Works	40
Treasure Island		17	Ivanhoe	14
Ivanhoe		12	Huckleberry Finn	9
Tarzan Series		11	Tom Sawyer	9
Huckleberry Finn		10	Treasure Island	9
Oliver Twist		10	River's End	7
When a Man's a Man		8	Laddie	6
Sea Hawk		7	Mark Twain	3
Tom Sawyer		7	Clansman	3
Call of the Wild		6	Tarzan Series	2
Mark Twain's Works		5	Penrod	2
Last of the Mohicans		4	Three Musketeers	2
Captain Blood		3	Kidnapped	2
Covered Wagon		3	Tale of Two Cities	2
Ben Hur		2	David Copperfield	2
Sherlock Holmes		2	Sherlock Holmes	2

86   CHILDREN'S INTERESTS IN READING

Trail of the Lonesome Pine	2	Call of the Wild	2
Red Rock	2	The Flirt	2
Last Days of Pompeii	2	Sea Hawk	2
Pathfinder	2	Hound of the Baskervilles	2

TABLE XXX
MOST POPULAR BOOKS. GREENSBORO
Girls

Number	87		127
Grade	VIII		IX
Anne of Green Gables	12	Zane Gray's Works	38
Nobody's Boy and Girl	7	Seventeen	25
Ben Hur	6	O. Henry Short Stories	21
Secret Garden	6	To have and to Hold	18
Kilarney of the Orchard	6	Little Women	18
Dorothy Dale Series	5	Freckles	17
Tom Sawyer	5	Trail of the Lonesome Pine	14
Lavender and Old Lace	4	Scaranouche	11
Old Fashion Girl	4	The Sheik	11
Pollyanna	4	Girl of the Limberlost	10
Girl of the Limberlost	4	Covered Wagon	10
Huckleberry Finn	3	Tom Sawyer	8
Freckles	3	Secret Garden	8
The Spy	3	Little Shepherd of Kingdom Come	6
Man Without a Country	3		
The Four Millions	3	Ben Hur	6
Treasure Island	3	Rebecca of Sunnybrook Farm	6
Zane Gray's Works	3	Red Pepper Burns	6
Little Shepherd of Kingdom Come	3	Lorna Doone	6
		Call of the Wild	5
Call of the Wild	3	Graustark Series	4
Mammy's White Folks	3	Laddie	4
Tale of Two Cities	2	Truxton King	4

Number	89		89
Grade	X		XI
Three Musketeers	14	O. Henry Short Stories	32
Virginian	12	Ben Hur	18
Little Minister	12	So Big	13
Tale of Two Cities	11	Lorna Doone	13
Zane Gray's Works	10	Little Women	13
Scaramouche	9	David Copperfield	11
Call of the Wild	8	Mill on the Floss	10
Girl Scout Series	8	To Have and to Hold	9
Little Minister	8	Zane Gray's Books	9

INVESTIGATIONS BY QUESTIONNAIRE

Book	Pts	Book	Pts
Rosary	7	Ivanhoe	9
Little Women	7	Tale of Two Cities	8
Secret Garden	7	Jane Eyre	7
So Big	7	Silas Marner	7
Covered Wagon	6	Rivals	7
Girl of the Limberlost	6	Last of the Mohicans	6
Ivanhoe	6	Covered Wagon	5
To Have and to Hold	6	Trail of the Lonesome Pine	5
House of the Five Swords	6	Shakespeare's Works	4
Treasure Island	5	Shepherd of the Hills	4
Anne of Green Gables	5	House of Five Swords	4

Table XXXI
Most Popular Books. Charlotte
Points = Sum of first, second, third, fourth, and fifth choices.

Girls

Number	187		171	
Grade	VIII	Points	IX	Points
Zane Gray's Works		80	Zane Gray's Works	74
Girl of the Limberlost		43	Girl of the Limberlost	55
Little Women		34	Graustark	41
Last of the Mohicans		21	Little Women	34
Little Colonel Series		21	Freckles	32
Pollyanna		20	Little Shepherd of Kingdom	
Secret Garden		20	Come	31
Anne of Green Gables		20	Anne of Green Gables	20
Seventeen		16	Covered Wagon	14
Laddie		15	Harvester	14
Freckles		13	Tarzan Series	13
Rebecca of Sunnybrook Farm		12	Tale of Two Cities	12
Little Men		12	Mammy's White Folks	11
Anne of Avonlea		12	Freckles	10
Huckleberry Finn		11	Rebecca of Sunnybrook Farm	10
Polly Series		10	Huckleberry Finn	10
Elsie Dinsmore		10	Laddie	9
Heidi		10	Autobiography of Helen Keller	9
Graustark Series		10	Ivanhoe	9
Penrod		9	Her Father's Daughter	9
			Circular Staircase	7

Number	105		92	
Grade	X		XI	
Zane Gray's Works		59	Zane Gray's Works	53
Girl of the Limberlost		35	Girl of the Limberlost	16
Silas Marner		22	Tale of Two Cities	13

Anne of Green Gables	16	Ivanhoe	11
Laddie	15	Graustark Series	9
Tale of Two Cities	13	Treasure Island	8
Graustark Series	12	The Rosary	8
Seventeen	9	Freckles	8
Her Father's Daughter	7	Secret Garden	7
Treasure Island	7	Circular Staircase	7
Little Shepherd of Kingdom Come	7	Her Father's Daughter	6
		Penrod	6
Just David	6	Pollyanna	6
Little Minister	6	St. Elmo	6
When a Man's a Man	6	Top of the World	6
Tom Sawyer	5	Anne of Green Gables	5
Ivanhoe	5	Twice Told Tales	5
Oliver Twist	5	When Knighthood was in Flower	5
Call of the Wild	4		
The Rosary	4	David Copperfield	4
Red Rock	4	Tom Sawyer	4

Looking more directly at Grade VIII we find too few boys in Greensboro to allow of a very reliable popularity list. Of the twelve listed in this table six appear in the corresponding grade list from Charlotte. Grade IX offers a fairer opportunity for comparison. Of the twenty books listed for Greensboro nine appear in Charlotte in the ninth grade, nine in the tenth grade, and ten in the eleventh grade. When we consider the girls similar results obtain with some slight differences. In Charlotte, Zane Gray leads by a safe margin in all four grades but in Greensboro his books lead only in Grade IX. There are many books the same in any two corresponding grades; for example, in the eighth grade seven out of twenty are identical; in the ninth, nine; in the tenth, nine; and in the eleventh only four. In the senior year the differences seem quite marked. In general it certainly seems striking that so many of the same books should appear on the corresponding lists of most popular books. Of course many of these books are on the required reading lists of these two high schools and would get a larger number of choices merely because they come to mind, but many of the others do not so appear.

Finally, by combining the results of the two investigations a list of popular books has been compiled based on a census of nearly five thousand high school pupils (Table XXXII). It would appear to be fairly representative of interests of high school boys and girls in books the country over.

TABLE XXXII

THE MOST POPULAR BOOKS FROM BOTH INVESTIGATIONS. 1917 AND 1925

Girls

Age	*12–13*		*14–16*		*17–18*
Number	434		1860		665
Girl of the Limberlost	32	Zane Gray's Works	252	Zane Gray's Works	71
Little Women	31	Little Women	123	Girl of the Limberlost	65
Pollyanna	29	Pollyanna	81	Tale of Two Cities	49
Zane Gray's Works	24	Freckles	81	David Copperfield	35
Freckles	23	Anne of Green Gables	67	Little Women	32
Little Colonel Series	18	Little Shepherd of Kingdom Come	53	Anne of Green Gables	26
Fairy Tales	17	Girl of the Limberlost	54	Shepherd of the Hills	25
Rebecca of Sunnybrook Farm	16	Laddie	51	Little Shepherd of Kingdom Come	25
Elsie Dinsmore	15	Graustark	42	Freckles	23
Laddie	14	O. Henry	40	When a Man's a Man	22
Anne of Green Gables	12	Seventeen	40	Ivanhoe	22
Boy Scout Series	10	Tale of Two Cities	40	Ben Hur	22
Little Pepper Series	8	To Have and to Hold	32	Trail of the Lonesome Pine	19
Ben Hur	7	Silas Marner	31	Call of the Wild	18
Secret Garden	7	Covered Wagon	30	Lorna Doone	18
Heidi	7	Scaramouche	26	O. Henry Stories	17
When Knighthood was in Flower	7	David Copperfield	24	Eyes of the World	16
Seventeen	6	Treasure Island	23	Lady of the Lake	14
Eight Cousins	5	Huckleberry Finn	19	Little Minister	14
Black Beauty	5	Virginian	18	Laddie	12

Boys

Number 311		1147		434	
Boy Scout Series	47	Zane Gray's Works	397	Zane Gray's Works	116
Zane Gray's Works	38	Call of the Wild	144	Call of the Wild	83
Call of the Wild	29	Treasure Island	110	Ivanhoe	42
Treasure Island	20	Tom Sawyer	104	Huckleberry Finn	42
Huckleberry Finn	18	Tarzan Series	78	Tom Sawyer	34
Tom Swift Series	14	Tom Swift Series	51	Treasure Island	33
Penrod	11	Penrod	47	Tale of Two Cities	31
Tom Sawyer	11	Covered Wagon	42	When a Man's a Man	28
Tarzan Series	7	Last of the Mohicans	40	Boy Scout Series	16
Driven from Home	6	Rover Boy Series	20	Trail of the Lonesome Pine	14
Rover Boy Series	6	White Fang	17	David Copperfield	14
Last of the Mohicans	6	Robinson Crusoe	16	Lorna Doone	13
Kidnapped	6	Boy Scout Series	15	Freckles	12
Motor Boy Series	6	Ivanhoe	14	Little Shepherd of Kingdom Come	12
Robinson Crusoe	5	Sea Hawk	13	Shepherd of the Hills	11
Billy Whiskers	5	Kazan	11	Lady of the Lake	11
Ivanhoe	4	O. Henry	11	White Fang	11
White Fang	4	Ben Hur	11	Tom Swift Series	11
Robin Hood	4	Kidnapped	11	Sea Hawk	10
Radio Boy Series	3	Huckleberry Finn	11	Tarzan Series	10

SUMMARY AND CONCLUSION

In this chapter, new data bearing on the preferences of pupils for books and magazines have been presented. The books and magazines have been classified into the same categories which were used in the former investigation, and most popular lists have been similarly constructed. Comparative tables both of magazines and books have been made from which one can draw definite conclusions as to the differences in choice, both between the results of the two investigations, and between the two cities of the present investigation. Moreover, in addition to the age groups of the former investigation, grade groups were used in this one so that lists of interesting books and magazines could be had for each grade.

INVESTIGATIONS BY QUESTIONNAIRE 91

In this investigation, just as in the former one, we see boys turning to books of adventure and to fiction. Humor also, expecially of the Mark Twain variety, has a great appeal for boys. It is true that some of the old favorites have given away to those of a later vintage; that the books of Zane Gray have displaced *The Call of the Wild* and *White Fang*, as the leading books when the number of votes aone is considered; but yet there is little change in the type of thing liked. The school, of course, plays its part here by displaying books of the better type, and by introducing them into its curriculum; and these books for these reasons undoubtedly receive higher rank in popularity lists than others. But, not infrequently, books introduced by the school are lightly passed over when actual interest is involved. Some differences do appear. Books of adventure appealed more strongly in the first investigation. This may have been due to the fact that about seventeen hundred of those formerly questioned were from beyond the Mississippi, and also from smaller municipalities; and yet 1800 in this enquiry were from Washington, D. C. It may be (and I suspect this reason more strongly) that there has been a change in the attitude towards fiction in the last few years which may be due to the greater development and patronage of the moving picture. And finally, boys read magazines dealing with science less today than formerly. It seems that the *American Magazine* has caught the boys' fancy and has pulled towards it much of the interest that formerly went elsewhere.

Girls of the two investigations read quite similar books. They stick to fiction at all times and in all places. Certainly a few more of them choose books of adventure and humor now than formerly. But otherwise they shy away from information, science, and history, like poetry a little, and now and then are captivated by a book of some great living heroine, such as Helen Keller. Girls of the more recent investigations seem to have a more mature taste and to have discarded some of the juvenile fiction. Their interest has also been caught by Zane Gray. Among magazines, fiction, woman's arts, and the pictorials hold the first place now as then. Adventure seems to have suffered a slump in the more recent study; and particularly during the years 12–16 there is more fiction liked. Again, it is the *American Magazine* that turns the scales, for it is chosen on almost all occasions. It is so widely liked that one could almost use this magazine as a symbol of high school interest in magazines. Magazines of humor received a larger number of votes in the present investigation.

Between the two cities of the present investigation a few differences in choices of books and magazines appear. In Greensboro, O. Henry's works are very popular, because the grownups of Greensboro make much of the fact that this literary man was born right there among them. In Charlotte, *The National Geographic* received a much larger vote than in Greensboro. In general there were many similarities between the two cities in the types of books and magazines chosen but only a few scattered differences.

CHAPTER V

INTERPRETATION AND ATTEMPTED EXPLANATION OF CHILDREN'S INTERESTS

THE INTERESTS IN READING OF BOYS, AGE 10-13 YEARS, TREATED FROM THE PSYCHOLOGICAL POINT OF VIEW

The question, Why do children like one book rather than another? is more difficult to answer. If the children are asked why, they give responses that are not trustworthy. The fact is, children do not know why, since they are driven on by instinctive forces of which they are little cognizant. It must be realized, in the first place, that these instincts do not function as they would have functioned, had they not been complicated by experiences of all kinds. The direction that an instinct takes, then, is determined by training and education. That there are original forces, remarkably alike in spite of these complications, is evidenced by the unusual similarity of choices of books by thousands of children.

From the standpoint of original nature, what are the chief drives impelling the boy to this type of reading?[1] Possibly the strongest drive at this age among the boys is love of sensory life for its own sake. This is evidenced by the multiplicity of experiences that the hero shares, in the rapid and sudden changes of scene, and in the vividness of detail necessary to attract the boy. It is considerably like the moving pictures with their rapid change of film, their glaring advertisements, but more mild. More concretely,

---

[1] Recent investigations have cast considerable doubt on the inheritance of many of Thorndike's "instincts." Even if they are not inherited they are certainly potent drives in determining interests.

the boy scout must wander through the woods, he must continually learn new things. A scout must move along from place to place; he must be in many battles; he must protect many defenseless people, and he must not fail in hair breadth escapes. The baseball player must make many hits; he must pitch many games; he must get into many scrapes. Is there description, it must be brief, and with a few bold lines the whole must be sketched, for there is no time for loitering as one must hurry on. Not style but action is the requisite. All of which characteristics depend in surprisingly large measure on the original attentiveness which finds satisfaction in sudden changes and sharp contrasts.

Another powerful incentive is rivalry. Not one of the popular books omits a description of that "increased vigor in man's activity where other men are engaged in the same activity and the satisfyingness of superiority to them." Truly the last clause is "sickled over with the pale caste" of outwardly more gentlemanly conduct, but even then there is a secret satisfaction in gaining the mastery. In making the college team we see it again and again, in becoming leader of the junior class some less fortunate individual must be removed from the scene of action. The hero indeed has better qualities—he is far more honorable, he never takes unfair advantage—all told he is quite the man for the place. Of course he is gentleman enough not to exult, but the satisfyingness is there all the same. In the Boy Scout Series this instinct is appealed to less, but it is necessarily present. The instincts of mastery and rivalry are so closely intertwined in the books for boys that it is best that they should be treated together. An individual is the rival of another largely because he wishes to gain the mastery. This instinct takes the form of mastery over an opponent in war or sports in some particular thing and the mere domination for its own sake is always condemned.

"Man is originally attentive .... to all the situations to which he has further tendencies to respond." (Thorndike, Vol. I.) That section of human nature between $11\frac{1}{2}$ and $13\frac{1}{2}$ certainly has a tendency to respond to wars and adventures imaginatively. The admiration of the boy of this age for outdoor sports and his participation in them leads them to attend further to their description in books, and his loyalty to the boy scouts causes him to respond to accounts of them in books. His present activities are reflected in great interest in magazines concerning aeroplanes, submarines, wireless, making birds' nests, kites, building houses, fashioning tents, solving puzzles, and conundrums, and in the enjoyment of magic and such like. During the late war there was an unusual interest in books dealing with war conditions and one might have unwittingly attributed this great interest in fighting to the influence of the boy's immediate environment. But he was interested in war and fighting before this war began, as the former and present popularity of Henty and Tomlinson, and others, attests. Undoubtedly the war accentuated and stimulated this interest but back of it all is that instinct of fighting. Also it might be maintained that the instinct of manipulation expresses itself and is directed into the making of birds' houses, tents, and such like. His everyday interest in puzzles is reflected in the popularity of books on puzzles.

To understand that kindliness is a driving force one must read the most gory of stories, for even here the savage chief cannot bear to see his noble rival destroyed. The hero's welfare is more important than the carrying on of the Indian's cause. In the school stories we see this kindliness flowing out upon all that are around the hero. He likes to see everybody happy. In fact, his main business in life is to make more people happy.

The instincts of "counter attack," "escape from restraint," "overcoming a moving obstacle," "irrational response to pain," "combat in rivalry," and "being thwarted," which together may be designated as the fighting instinct, play a tremendous part in the life of the boys. Just how much, one can understand by glancing at the titles of books which catch and hold the interest. Altsheler, Tomlinson, or Henty, and many others of like nature are popular in every library. Boys imaginatively fight the hero's battles with him, they are breathless when he is entangled in a death struggle with some powerful and despicable enemy. In a milder form and mixed with rivalry we see the fighting instinct playing a large part in school sports. The hero must enter into several fisticuffs before his prestige is established, but he must always fight for the right. In the Boy Scouts there are many characteristics resembling military organizations, yet there is little appeal to the fighting instinct. But even here Don Strong must assert his leadership at the expense of the bully who makes life miserable for him, and a real battle ensues. In the books for boys one is not surprised at finding a considerable sprinkling of fights. The contrast between the books read by boys and those read by girls is here most sharp: the boys' books being filled with fighting, self-assertion, and strenuous rivalry; the girls' books with kindliness, self-forgetfulness and mild rivalry.

The boys' heroes are not so susceptible to approval and scornful behavior as are those of the girls. They are apt to care less about what people think and to go ahead, driven rather by the instinct of mastery. Nevertheless, Don Strong enjoys the commendation of the scout leader as well as the plaudits of his comrades. He fears the jibes of his friend. The brother of a hero feels downcast indeed when suspicion of wrongdoing has been skillfully directed toward him by an enemy. In one case a miscreant suddenly disappeared from school because moral opprobrium was his lot. The Scout's commendation of the younger lad makes the latter cheerful for many a day. Illustrations of this could be multiplied to an almost endless extent. On the other hand, the hero directs his approval to those who deserve it by being strong, honest, and open, and his scorn against the opposite. Scorn, however, rarely is becoming to a real hero and is not dwelt upon. Greed, teasing, tormenting, bullying, envy, and jealousy are unreservedly condemned.

The drives concomitant with the instincts of "multiform mental activity" and of "multiform physical activity" may properly be considered together since the chief joy of life comes in the mental control over physical activity. The joy of mental control comes in the control over a game of baseball, or over the building of a tent, or over shooting unerringly. The hero's greatest happiness is in that self-control in those situations which makes him independent not of others but of others in doing that particular thing he sets out to do. Complicated with this is the drive of mastery. When he is no longer rattled if his team is behind, or flurried when an Indian is beyond a nearby tree, he gets the fullest satisfaction. The higher types of mental activity are not emphasized except now and then by some wise scoutmaster or perspicacious teacher.

The most important drives have already been mentioned, but there remain a few instincts important enough to deserve brief mention. In this group perhaps the most important is the gregarious instinct which is appealed to again and again. The hero must have friends. When he walks out alone, except on rare occasions he misses the comradeship of his fellows. He is happiest when surrounded by his team, or by his Boy Scout comrades, or by his admiring school.

What then are the great satisfiers of boyhood at this age as expressed in the heroes of the books they read? Below is a list of the most important ones:

The chief *Satisfiers* deduced from a study of books frequently chosen:
  Physical strength and aptitude.
  Self-control, particularly in critical situations.
  Independence based on actuality.
  Making a team at the expense of an unjust rival.
  Saving a person's life.
  Gaining the mastery in a physical combat when the opponent is despicable.
  Being loyal.
  Going somewhere.
  Having new experiences of almost any kind.
  Gaining the plaudits of his fellows.
  Being honest, straightforward, open, trustworthy.
  Winning admiration, even of an enemy, in these things.
Annoyers: The opposites of the above would in almost every case be annoying.

The Interests in Reading of Girls, Age 10–13 Years Treated from the Psychological Point of View

The fighting instinct on the one hand and the maternal instinct on the other are the most potent causes of the differences between the reading of boys and girls at this period. The instinct "to nurse, to care for and fuss over others, to relieve, comfort, and console" is expressed again and again in the heroines of the books. Any failure to relieve or comfort is unreservedly condemned. Not only is the mother in *Little Women* willing to give up her breakfast, but even the young and at times thoughtless daughters comprehend that it would also give them pleasure to give up their breakfast. Out of sheer good fellowship the girls like to cheer the lonely two next door. It is real fun to carry flowers to a sick individual in the neighborhood. In *Peggy* the heart of the western girl is wrung at the sight of her oppressed fellow classman. The author skillfully puts the reader in a mood receptive to such kindness and the girls evidently like it. There are few heroines who show more of this instinct than Rebecca of Sunnybrook Farm. She helps out the neighboring poor families in every way that she can. Even the hero of the story shows in a large degree this quality so liked by girls. He is one of the trustees of a girls' school and brings presents to all the children of his neighboring town. Hans Brinker is kindness itself. Clover of the story of *The High Valley* is all one could ask in love and kindness to her neighbors. Katrina in the story of that name enjoys helping others and her fond aunt is much praised for her kindness and philanthropy. Burnett's Sara Crewe, though hungry, gives away her rolls to the street waif who is near starvation. This story is full of thoughtfulness for others. In sampling and reading these books these facts forced themselves upon me again and again. Sometimes even where these characteristics are almost apotheosized—as in the Elsie Dinsmore Series (not in the libraries)—the books are still extremely popular. This type of thing is what the girls call a "nice story." This maternal instinct is so closely akin to kindliness that what has been said of the former would also apply to the latter.

Attention and interest in sharp contrasts and sudden changes are not nearly so evident as is the case with books for boys. In fact the opposite is often the case. In *Anne of Green Gables*, for instance, the action is rather slow. Anne likes to sit and dream of the cherry and apple blossoms. The action in every case is not nearly so rapid. We have more time to get thoroughly acquainted with the intimate details of everyday life, particularly of the home and neighborhood, as well as with the desires and aspirations of the heroines. The interest in visual exploration often takes the form of a trip to the city where the gay people, handsome clothes, and magnificent equipages rather startle but tremendously attract the girl. If, as in *The Little Gray House*, a girl takes interest in manipulating a mechanical situation, it is because of her needy parent and her love of her dreamy father.

The joy of being together is best exemplified in school stories, although the joys of the large family are exemplified in such books as *The Little Gray House, Five Little Peppers and How They Grew*, or *Little Women*, and the joylessness of life without them, in *Rebecca of Sunnybrook Farm*. When Rebecca was settled in a much more comfortable but less joyous home she missed the peasures of her former home associations. This longing for fellowship with others of like nature is so universally expressed that it needs no further comment.

The responses to approval and to scornful behavior show themselves particularly in the unusual interest of the heroines in dress, for with the women mentioned, dress brings approval both of their own sex and of the other. The girls in *Little Women* are so much concerned about their clothes that one is treated to half a chapter which relates in minute detail how they patched here, covered up there, prepared to keep their backs to the wall, that their clothes might be presentable. And when one of the girls went to a fashionable country home her little hostess was so chagrined at the simple dress of her guest that she contrived to get her visitor to wear one of her own. Rebecca had a great struggle with her aunts to get her some presentable dresses. This very method was used also in *Katrina* when the heroine went to the city. The good breeding of the heroine's friends always prevents them from displaying toward such dresses a scorn which others would not be slow in showing. These small aside-looks of scorn used by women in these stories are often sufficient to send the poor heroine upstairs weeping. Externally they often meet scorn with scorn but inwardly nothing seems to hurt so much as to be thought ill-dressed and consequently poor. Even when these girls are scorned because of inelegant clothes, they tacitly admit to themselves that the scorners are right. On the other hand, the softened scorn of their elders in regard to their slovenliness and carelessness is met with an acquiescence which contains considerable opposition and oftentimes rebellion.

The fact that girls are more interested in the sort of clothes they wear at this age is one of the evidences of the greater response to the attention of human beings. If a boy —as in Altsheler—decides upon a certain course, he goes ahead, thinking and caring little for what others think. Not so with the girls. They must consider what father thinks, what mother thinks, and, at least in stories, are always influenced strongly by the opinions of these people. The mere fact that so many popular books treat of kindliness and good fellowship, of self-sacrifice and of noble giving shows that girls are more interested in these things than are boys.

The instinct of shyness manifests itself in a variety of ways. In *The Little Gray House* the heroine is indescribably shy and faint when she is about to interview her father's old friend. Again she is almost struck speechless when she must meet the directors of a business concern in order to explain the intricacies of her father's invention. But—what girls must like—she fights off this feeling and remembering that she is her father's daughter launches forth into a masterly description of the machine. On the negative side Jo in *Little Women* felt almost none of that shyness in the presence of strangers. Peggy felt a sinking of the heart when face to face with her principal. Sometimes this shyness is overcome by the magnanimous act of the girl's superior, expressed perhaps by a kind word or a friendly pat. Soon the girl feels at home even in the most unusual circumstances.

The instinct of rivalry is, of course, often directed under the author's hand into rivalry in unselfishness, kindliness, thoughtfulness, etc. Sometimes, as in *Peggy*, it is a rivalry for leadership in the class; as in *Little Women*, a competition for the greatest kindliness to each other and to others; as in *Rebecca*, for the good graces of the teacher; or as in *Hans Brinker*, in order to win a skating race. All told, this instinct plays, in comparison with rivalry in boys' books, only a very small part.

Teasing and tormenting express themselves most consistently in gossip and sneers. In school pranks, however, they may take on a physical aspect. In every case the authors condemn them unreservedly.

Generally speaking, the emotions play a much larger part in girls' stories. Girls permit themselves to give expression to their feelings more frequently. Nor do they mind a bit of crying. It is joy and happiness one day and grief and sorrow the next. One is struck by this difference. The younger girls in the story are always more easily affected than are boys of the same age in boys' stories.

The chief great *Satisfiers* of girls of age 10–13, as shown by their reading, are these:

Kindliness to others, especially to those who are in distress.
To wear beautifully tailored clothes.
To hold her position socially as high as any one.
In being honorable and possessing a clean mind.
In unsefishness.
In being useful in the home.
In playing pranks at school.
In being honest at school.
In gaining the esteem of those worth while at school.
In being loved and admired for onesself.
In protecting those weaker.
In having things happen.

In being open and not deceitful.
In getting a box from home, in having a feast till late hours, and in telling stories.
In success in dramatics.
In going to a city, if raised in the country.
Annoyers: The opposites of these usually annoy.

During the years 13 to 18 the sex instinct in addition to those instincts already mentioned becomes potent. It manifests itself in the increasing amount of adult fiction chosen by both boys and girls.

The sex instinct is only slightly evident in the reading of boys up to 12–13 years, but after this age-group its manifestations in the liking for adult fiction are increasingly apparent. The impulses of mastery, rivalry, and fighting continue very strong throughout the high school age. They are expressed in the large number of books of adventure chosen by boys. Thus the interest of boys in adult fiction and in adventure is a direct outgrowth of their original nature.

In girls the sex instinct manifests itself as early as the eleventh year. But at 12–13 this instinct makes itself felt in a large percentage of their total reading and from 14–16 it becomes the dominant force in determining the type of reading liked. The maternal instinct and the kindliness of the earlier years are reinforced by the sex impulse with a result that at least 85 per cent of the total number of books very much liked is composed of adult and juvenile fiction. That the instinct of kindliness is still powerful throughout these years is evidenced by the popularity among girls of *Little Women* and *Pollyanna*—books in which the slight thread of the love story is dominated by the emphasis placed on the happiness of others.

www.ingramcontent.com/pod-product-compliance
Lightning Source LLC
Chambersburg PA
CBHW030117010526
44116CB00005B/281